Serial Killer Quote of the Day

365 Days of Serial Killers Uncut and In Their Own Words

by johnny trevisani

This book is a journey into the minds of serial killers and mass murderers.

The information which follows is disturbing. It is provided for education and informational purposes only, without expressed or implied warranty of any kind, including warranties of accuracy, completeness, or fitness for any particular purpose. Neither the author, nor the publisher are responsible for misuse of the material, nor for any psychological or emotional discomfort caused by the material. You understand that you are using any and all information available in this book at your own risk.

Enjoy.

Table of Contents

January

January's featured serial killer is Jeffrey Dahmer.

Jeffrey Dahmer was a really weird guy. He was a really scary one too. No other name in modern history conjures up disturbing images like that of Jeffrey Dahmer. Even for a serial killer Dahmer is reviled. Mention his name to anyone and they will most likely recoil with horror and indignance.

Known as the Milwaukee Cannibal for his ritualistic dismemberment and cannibalization of his victims, Dahmer terrorized Milwaukee from the late 1970s until he was captured and convicted in the early 1990s.

A closeted homosexual, Jeffrey struggled with his own sexual identity, hiding his desires from his disapproving parents. Many of his victims were homosexual men whom Jeffrey met, had sex with, then murdered . He often had sex with the corpses. Later, Dahmer would do experiments on his victims, to try to keep them around forever. When this failed he would chop them up and cook them. He often kept their heads, and stored them around his apartment.

Dahmer was diagnosed as suffering from borderline personality disorder. Often his world of fantasy and reality blurred as he acted out sexual fantasies involving dominance and control. His victims became tools of his macabre fantasy world, ultimately ending with death and cannibalism.

During his reign of terror, Dahmer was suspected to be responsible for seventeen deaths and was convicted for the murder of fifteen people. If it weren't for one victim's escape, who knows how long he would have continued his murder rampage?

Dahmer was sentenced to fifteen consecutive life sentences, but was beaten to death with a metal bar in a prison bathroom by a fellow inmate after serving only three years. He was killed by convicted murderer Christopher Scarver. According to Scarver, Dahmer had been taunting other inmates by constructing "severed limbs" out of food and ketchup.

January 1

"My refrigerator broke and the meat spoiled."

What Jeffrey Dahmer told neighbors when they complained of the stench emanating from his apartment, which contained the remains of his dismembered victims.

Name: Jeffrey Dahmer
Nickname: The Milwaukee Cannibal; The Milwaukee Monster
Killings: 17
Location: Wisconsin
Years Active: 1978-1991
Fun Fact: Dahmer wanted to turn his victims into his own personal zombies.

January 2

"I'm not the kind of person who socialized a lot. There was no way to let off steam."

Name: Ted Bundy
Killings: 30-36+
Location: Washington
Years active: 1961-1978
Fun Fact: Bundy managed to escape from custody twice.

January 3

"I am a mistake of nature. I deserve to be done away with."

Name: Andrei Chikatilo
Nickname: The Butcher of Rostov; The Red Ripper; The Forest Strip Killer; The Rostov Ripper
Killings: 53-56+
Location: Russia
Years active: 1978-1990
Fun Fact: Chikalito was a teacher and had a degree in Russian Literature.

January 4

"I could hardly go anywhere but women would want to talk to me; it wasn't me who did the chasing. Girls were attracted to me."

Name: John Christie
Nickname: The Rillington Place Strangler
Killings: 8
Location: England
Years active: 1943-1953
Fun Fact: Christie initially claimed his victims came to his house and pestered him for sex.

January 5

"Before you know it I had put my arm around her and that was it."

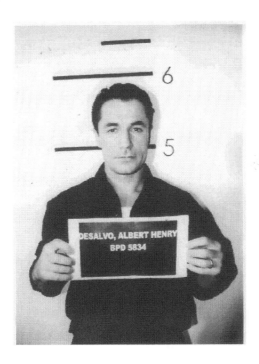

Name: Albert DeSalvo
Nickname: The Boston Strangler
Killings: 13
Location: Boston, MA
Years active: 1962-1964
Fun Fact: Desalvo would introduce himself to women as a representative of a modeling agency.

January 6

"The white man is my enemy, and I will fight to gain my manhood or die trying."

Name: Mark James Robert Essex
Killings: 9
Location: New Orleans, LA
Years active: 1972-1973
Fun Fact: Japanese metal band Church of Misery wrote a song about Essex called "Soul Discharge."

January 7

"What a thrill that will be if I have to die in the electric chair. It will be the supreme thrill, the only one I haven't tried."

Name: Albert Fish
Nickname/AKA: Thomas Frank Howard
Killings: 10+
Location: New York
Years active: 1924-1932
Fun Fact: When Fish was electrocuted the chair short circuited.

January 8

"It was like a release. I'd feel like I lost twenty pounds."

(Explaining how it felt to kill someone)

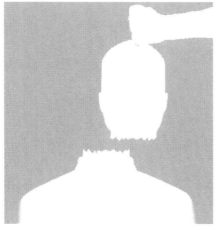

(no pic available)

Name: Joe Fischer
Killings: 2-40+
Location: United States
Years active: 1953-1979
Fun Fact: Fischer's mother was a prostitute.

January 9

"I should never have been convicted of anything more serious than running a cemetery without a license."

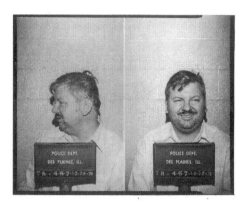

Name: John Wayne Gacy
Nickname: The Killer Clown
Killings: 34
Location: Illinois
Years active: 1972-1978
Fun Fact: At one point, Gacy managed a Kentucky Fried Chicken franchise. He insisted that his staff call him "The Colonel."

January 10

"Society owes me a wife and family. I want to get ten women and keep them here and get them all pregnant. Then, when they have babies, I want to raise those children here too. We'll be one big happy family."
(Philadelphia's Cellar of Horror Murderer, 1986)

Name: Gary Heidnik
Nickname: Brother Bishop
Killings: 2+
Location: Philadelphia
Years active: 1986-1987
Fun Fact: Heidnik had an IQ of 130, indicating someone of high intelligence.

January 11

"For Heaven's sake, catch me before I kill more. I cannot control myself."

Name: William Heirens
Nickname: The Lipstick Killer
Killings: 3
Location: Illinois
Years active: 1945-1946
Fun Fact: Heirens was known as the Lipstick Killer because he scrawled a message in lipstick. He also was a good ballroom dancer.

January 12

"I have commenced to assume the form and features of the Evil One himself."

Name: H.H. Holmes
Nickname/AKA: Dr. Henry Holmes
Killings: 27-200
Location: United States
Years active: 1888-1894
Fun Fact: The first time Holmes was arrested it was for horse swindling.

January 13

"I have got the book, I know how many you have to do..."

Name: Colin Ireland
Nickname: The Gay Slayer
Killings: 5
Location: England
Years active 1993
Fun Fact: Ireland claimed to be straight but met all of his victims, who were all male, in gay clubs.

January 14

"God placed me here to kill all whores."

(no pic available)

Name: Jack the Ripper (unknown)
Nickname: Jack the Ripper; The Whitechapel Murderer
Killings: 5+
Location: England
Years active: 1888-1891
Fun Fact: He killed only in the early morning hours and weekends.

January 15

"Wherever I go, people died."

Name: Helene Jegado
Killings: 36+
Location: France
Years active: 1833-1851
Fun Fact: Jegado was a domestic servant who apparently did not like a lot of her working conditions. She was beheaded in 1851.

January 16

"I don't mind people getting hurt because I just like to watch it."

Name: Walter Kelbach
Killings: 6
Location: Utah
Years active: 1966
Fun Fact: Kelbach killed people with his gay lover Myron Lance,
who was also his cousin.

January 17

"I have fantasies about mass murder... [I] made passionate love to their dead corpses. Taking life away from them... and then having possession of everything that used to be theirs. All that would be mine. Everything."

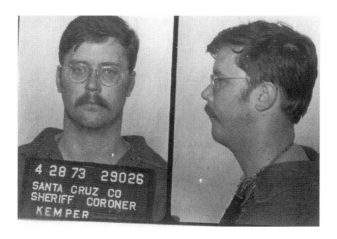

Name: Ed Kemper
Nickname: The Co-Ed Killer
Killings: 10
Location: California
Years active: 1964-1973
Fun Fact: After Kemper killed his mother, he tried to put her larynx in the garbage disposal but it spit it back up. He said this was appropriate seeing how she verbally abused him.

January 18

"Lonely widower seeking female companionship."
(Personal ad left in newspapers to attract new victims)

Name: Bela Kiss
Killings: 24+
Location: Hungary
Years active: 1900-1914
Fun Fact: Kiss was never caught.

January 19

"After my head has been chopped off, will I still be able to hear, at least for a moment, the sound of my own blood gushing from the stump of my neck? That would be the pleasure to end all pleasures."

Name: Peter Kurten
Nickname: The Dusseldorf Vampire; The Dusseldorf Monster
Killings: 9-60
Location: Germany
Years active: 1913-1929
Fun Fact: Kurten's father sexually abused his mother and sisters, which Kurten witnessed.

January 20

"Is every smoking chimney and every bad smell proof that a body is being burned?"

Name: Henri Desire Landru
Nickname: The Bluebeard of Gambais
Killings: 11
Location: France
Years active: 1915-1919
Fun Fact: Henri Desire Landru's severed head is on display at the Museum of Death in Hollywood, California.

January 21

"I don't have any towards the victims."

(speaking of feelings)

Name: Myron Lance
Killings: 6
Location: Utah
Years active: 1966
Fun Fact: Lance was the boyfriend of Walter Kelbach (January 16).

January 22

"You're all a bunch of feminists! I hate feminists!"

Name: Marc Lepine
Killings: 13
Location: Quebec
Year active: 1989
Fun Fact: Lepine bought his mother a present four days before his murders.

January 23

"I think it was just the hands doing it. I know a lot of things we done, in human sight, are impossible to believe."

Name: Henry Lee Lucas
Nickname: The Confession Killer
Killings: 3+
Location: United States (scattered)
Years active: 1960-1983
Fun Fact: Lucas became a born again Christian in prison and was a model prisoner.

January 24

"Don't treat the dogs like people. Treat the dogs like dogs. They are better than people."

Name: Charles Manson
Killings: 5
Location: California
Years active: 1971
Fun Fact: The Beach Boys recorded a song written by Manson "Never Learn Not to Love."

January 25

"I'm no average killer. I only got five hundred off the Dowling woman, but take Mrs. Jane Thompson, I took six thousand off of her."

Name: Raymond Martinez
Nickname: Lonely Hearts Bandit
Killings: 5-17
Location: New York
Years active: 1947-1949
Fun Fact: Martinez said he could control women through voodoo.

January 26

"I wrecked trains because I like to see people die. I like to hear them scream. I like to see them suffer."

Name: Sylvestre Matuschka
Killings: 22
Location: Germany
Years active: 1931
Fun Fact: It has been reported he would have an orgasm when he caused trains to crash.

January 27

"All of them were suffering and all of them were great nuisances. So I got rid of them."

Name: Frederick Mors
Nickname: Herr Doktor
Killings: 8
Location: New York
Years active: 1914-1915
Fun Fact: After arrest and incarceration Mors escaped, and was never heard from again.

January 28

"Murder is an act of love."

Name: Herbert Mullin
Killings: 13
Location: California
Years active: 1972-1973
Fun Fact: Mullin was voted "Most Likely to Succeed" in high school.

January 29

"I've killed so many I'm unable to remember them all."

Name: Arnfinn Nesset
Killings: 22
Location: Norway
Years active: 1977-1980
Fun Fact: Nesset killed many of his victims while being employed as the director of a nursing home.

January 30

"I have slain my own dragon."

Name: Dennis Nilsen
Nickname: The Kindly Killer
Killings: 15
Location: England
Years active: 1978-1983
Fun Fact: Nilsen was caught after his disposal of entrails clogged the drains of his house.

January 31

"In my lifetime I have murdered 21 human beings, I have committed thousands of burglaries, robberies, larcenies, arsons and last but not least I have committed sodomy on more than 1,000 male human beings. For all these things, I am not in the least bit sorry."

Name: Carl Panzram
Nickname/AKA: Jefferson Davis
Killings: 22
Location: United States (scattered)
Years active: 1915-1929
Fun Fact: Future U.S. President William H. Taft, when acting as Secretary of War, signed the papers to have Carl Panzram sent to Leavenworth Prison. Panzram later broke into Taft's home and stole Taft's personal gun. He used that stolen .45 Colt automatic to murder ten men. He was hung on September 5th, 1930.

February

February's featured serial killer is Edmund Kemper.

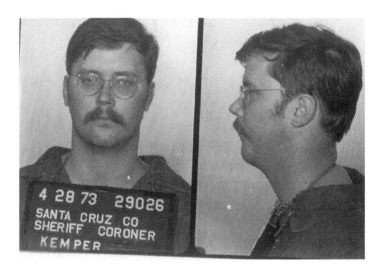

      Edmund Kemper or "Big Ed," as some called him, was massive. His towering and oppressive 6'9" 300lb frame played home to one of the most twisted and disturbed minds of modern times. Big Ed Kemper, known as the "Co-Ed Killer" by the press, terrorized the surrounding communities of Santa Cruz, California during the 1960s and early 1970s. In the end, Big Ed was responsible for ten, gruesomely disturbing murders involving dismemberment. Ed would have fun with his victim's bodies, performing acts of necrophilia with their body parts.

Growing up, Ed lived a normal life in southern California with his parents and sister. That is, if by normal you mean burying pets alive and living out bizarre sexual fantasies with his sister's dolls. Although Kemper often kept to himself, he was said to have a genius-level IQ; one report put his IQ at 136 to 145. But somewhere in that colossal frame his warped mind took control and created one of history's most ghastly serial killers.

Ed's tumultuous home life was made difficult by his parent's divorce and his mother's alcoholism. The Kemper family wasn't all that nurturing and loving. His sister tried to drown Ed in their pool. His mother, who was said to have been diagnosed with borderline personality disorder, would lock him in the basement. Ed, not loving the way his home life was with his mother, ran away, eventually landing with his dad. When Ed arrived at his dad's he unfortunately discovered his dad had remarried and fathered another son.

Ed really couldn't catch a break.

Ed then landed in Central California after his mom wouldn't let him back to live with her. It was while he was living with his grandparents during his adolescent years that Ed found his taste for killing, starting with killing and dismembering neighborhood pets to, at age fifteen, murdering his grandmother because he "just wondered how it would feel just to shoot Grandma." He killed his grandfather when he returned home because Kemper figured his grandfather would be angry with him for killing his wife.

After serving five short years in a mental facility, Kemper was released to his mother's custody. Then Big Ed hit his stride.

Kemper went on to murder six Co-Eds.

Ed ended his killing spree by killing his mother and his mother's friend. Kemper severed his mother's head, had sex with her skull, then cut out her vocal chords and put the vocal chords in the garbage disposal. He confessed to killing his mother and her friend, waited in his car calmly by a phone booth and was taken, without incident, into custody.

As of this writing, Big Ed is still alive, living out his days in the general population in the California Medical Facility in California.

February 1

**"Society's had their chance. I'm going hunting.
Hunting humans."**

Name: James Oliver Huberty
Nickname/AKA: San Ysidro Massacre Killer
Killings: 21
Location: California
Years active: 1984
Fun Fact: Huberty had a license for embalming.

February 2

"She told everyone she was having sexual intercourse with me, in fact I decline this honor."

Name: Dr. Marcel Andre Petiot
Nickname: Doctor Satan
Killings: 27-63
Location: France
Years active: 1926-1944
Fun Fact: Petiot was discharged from the army after shooting himself in the foot. Later, he became the mayor of Villeneuve-sur-Yonne.

February 3

"Big deal. Death always went with the territory. See you in Disneyland."

(Upon receiving the death sentence at his trial)

Name: Richard Ramirez
Nickname: The Night Stalker
Killings: 14
Location: California
Years active: 1984-1985
Fun Fact: Ramirez left an AC/DC baseball hat at the scene of a crime by mistake.

February 4

"There are forces that move in this world, forces you rarely see with the natural eye. I have seen the supernatural beings of darkness reaching for me. Oh God! They never stop reaching for all of us."

Name: Danny Rolling
Nickname: The Gainesville Murderer; The Gainesville Ripper
Killings: 8
Location: Florida
Years active: 1989-1990
Fun Fact: Rolling sang at his execution. He was executed in the same death chamber as Ted Bundy.

February 5

"I wish I had stayed in bed."

Name: Michael R. Ryan
Killings: 17
Location: England
Years active: 1987
Fun Fact: Radiohead's song "Sulk" was written in response to Ryan's killings.

February 6

"I'm just going down the road to meet the man that's going to buy you."

(Telling his first abductee)

Name: Gerard Schaefer
Nickname/AKA: Jerry Shepard
Killings: 2-30+
Location: Florida
Years active: 1969-1973
Fun Fact: Schaefer was a police officer at one point. He was fired after one month.

February 7

"You may take my life for what it is worth, but grant those I love peace and happiness."

Name: John Martin Scripps
Nickname: The Garden City Butcher
Killings: 3+
Location: Singapore
Years active: 1995
Fun Fact: Scripps was the first Westerner to be hung in Singapore for murder.

February 8

"One more, many more in store."

(Note left on the body of one of a victim)

(no pic available)

Name: Norman Afzal Simons
Nickname: The Station Strangler
Killings: 22
Location: South Africa
Years active: 1986-1994
Fun Fact: Simons, whose victims were young boys, was a teacher.

February 9

"We'll return this evening to say our formal goodbyes."

Name: George Joseph Smith
Nickname: Brides in the Bath Murderer
Killings: 3
Location: England
Years active: 1912-1915
Fun Fact: George Smith only had one legitimate job before becoming a con man and murderer. He was a baker.

February 10

"At least you made up your mind."

(Said to a juror after being found guilty.)

Name: Morris Solomon
Nickname: The Sacramento Slayer
Killings: 7
Location: California
Years active: 1986-1987
Fun Fact: Solomon reported "finding" his first victim's body to the police.

February 11

"If they only knew how much fun I was having in here, they would turn me loose."

Name: Richard Speck
Nickname/AKA: Richard Lindberg
Killings: 8
Location: Illinois
Years active: 1966
Fun Fact: Speck had a job as a meat delivery driver. He was fired after having six accidents in three months of work.

February 12

"Nighttime is when it gets really good... you get ready."

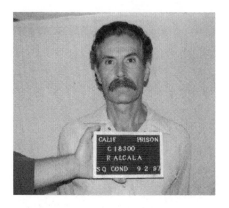

Name: Rodney James Alcala
Nickname: The Dating Game Killer
Killings: 8 - 130
Location: United States (scattered)
Years active: 1971-1979
Fun Fact: He appeared on the game show "The Dating Game" in 1978. He was picked by bachelorette Cheryl Bradshaw, but she refused to go on the date because she thought he was "creepy."

February 13

"There is no happiness without tears; no life without death. Beware, I will give you cause to weep."

(no pic available)

Name: Lucian Staniak
Nickname: The Red Spider
Killings: 6-20
Location: Poland
Years active: 1964-1967
Fun Fact: Staniak was an artist of sorts and was a member of "The Art Lovers Club." He killed two models that sat for the artists.

February 14

"The more I looked at people, the more I hated them."

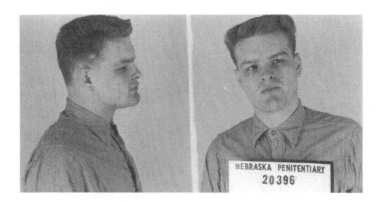

Name: Charles Starkweather
Nickname: Badlands Killer
Killings: 11 + 2 dogs
Location: Wyoming, Nebraska
Years active: 1957-1958
Fun Fact: In all of his murders Starkweather was accompanied by his 14 year old girlfriend, Caril Fugate.

February 15

"That is the trouble with society today - people are motivated by greed and there are no moral values at all."

Name: Peter Sutcliffe
Nickname: The Yorkshire Ripper
Killings: 13
Location: England
Years active: 1975-1980
Fun Fact: Sutcliffe claimed his motive for killing was the "Word of God."

February 16

"Just like the Mexican that wasn't going to let me out of the house. I took an axe and chopped him all up. What made me... I've been meaning to ask you... that time when I cooked some of these people? Why'd I do that?"

Name: Ottis Toole
Killings: 6+
Location: Florida
Years active: 1975-1983
Fun Fact: Toole was an accomplice of Henry Lee Lucas.

February 17

"I took the right leg of that woman's body, from the knee to the hip, took the fat off and ate it while I stared at the other girl. When I bit into it she just urinated right there."

Name: Arthur John Shawcross
Nickname: The Genesee River Killer
Killings: 14
Location: New York
Years active: 1972-1989
Fun Fact: Shawcross was married 4 times, but his wives all left him.

February 18

"I envisioned my mother in front of me, and I killed her."

Name: Jack Unterweger
Nickname: Jack the Writer; The Vienna Strangler
Killings: 12+
Location: Austria, Los Angeles
Years active: 1974-1992
Fun Fact: Unterweger was a published author of short stories, poems, plays, and an autobiography.

February 19

"Women are evil!"

Name: Coral Eugene Watts
Nickname: The Sunday Morning Slasher
Killings: 22-100
Location: United States
Years active: 1974-1982
Fun Fact: Watts is suspected of killing more than 100 women, which would make him the most prolific serial killer in American history.

February 20

"I hope you will forgive me. I asked for God's forgiveness and He gave it to me."

Name: Henry Louis Wallace
Nickname: The Taco Bell Strangler
Killings: 10
Location: North Carolina
Years active: 1990-1994
Fun Fact: Wallace used to be a radio DJ and was known as "Night Rider" for his smooth, sexy voice.

February 21

"l am prepared to die. After my death, I wish an autopsy on me to be performed to see if there is any mental disorder."

(From a note found after the killings)

Name: Charles Whitman
Nickname: The Texas Tower Sniper
Killings: 16
Location: Austin, Texas
Years active: 1966
Fun Fact: Whitman's autopsy revealed he had a brain tumor.

February 22

"I couldn't stop the killing, it got easier each time."

Name: William George Bonin
Nickname: The Freeway Killer
Killings: 36
Location: California
Years active: 1979-1980
Fun Fact: Bonin received social security benefits while on Death
Row.

February 23

"Many people have died for a good cause. I think these people may not have died in vain."

Name: Albert DeSalvo
Nickname: The Boston Strangler
Killings: 13
Location: Boston, MA
Years active: 1962-1964
Fun Fact: DeSalvo was never officially charged as the Boston Strangler. He died in prison while being held for other charges.

February 24

"I preferred young boys because they are better looking and have soft skin. And the priest said that children automatically go to heaven if they die before they're thirteen. So I know I did them a favor by sending them to heaven."

Name: Marcelo Costa de Andrade
Nickname: The Vampire of Niterói
Killings: 14
Location: Brazil
Years active: 1991
Fun Fact: De Andrade would drink the blood of his victims in order to become "as beautiful as them."

February 25

"I didn't want to hurt them, I only wanted to kill them."

Name: David Berkowitz
Nickname: Son of Sam
Killings: 6
Location: New York City
Years active: 1976-1977
Fun Fact: Berkowitz became obsessed with his downstairs neighbor. Here is an excerpt of a letter he wrote to him: "Craig Glassman, the cruelest sickest man on earth. Die Craig Die."

February 26

"We serial killers are your sons, we are your husbands. We are everywhere. And there will be more of your dead tomorrow."

Name: Ted Bundy
Killings: 30-36+
Location: United States (scattered)
Years active: 1969 (possibly as early as 1961) -1978
Fun Fact: Governor of Washington State, Daniel J. Evans wrote Ted Bundy a personal letter of recommendation. Bundy traveled with Evans on the campaign trail, working as a campaign aide responsible for recording stump speeches.

February 27

"I felt like a partisan."

(Speaking of the excitement he felt after killing an early victim)

Name: Andrei Chikatilo
Nickname: The Butcher of Rostov; The Red Ripper; The Forest Strip
Killer; The Rostov Ripper
Killings: 53-56+
Location: Soviet Union
Years active: 1978-1990
Fun Fact: Chikatilo was born in Ukraine during a time of famine.
When he was 5, he was told by his mother that she suspected his
older brother had been killed and eaten by neighbors.

February 28

"I Only Ate The Biceps! It Takes Me An Hour To Boil A Guy's Head!"

Name: Jeffrey Dahmer
Nickname: The Milwaukee Cannibal; The Milwaukee Monster
Killings: 17
Location: Wisconsin
Years active: 1978-1991
Fun Fact: The graphic novel "My Friend Dahmer" is written by one of Dahmer's high school friends.

February 29 (Leap Year)

**"I saw him... at peace in my armchair. I remember
wishing he could stay in peace like that forever. I had a
feeling of easing his burden with my strength."**

Name: Dennis Nilsen
Nickname: The Kindly Killer
Killings: 15
Location: England
Years active: 1978-1983
Fun Fact: Nilsen adored his grandmother.

March

March's featured serial killer is: H.H. Holmes

In Chicago, in the late 1880s, just in time for the world's fair, a hotel was built. It was a massive structure, built from three lots in the Englewood section of Chicago. The hotel, when opened was called: The World's Fair Hotel. Soon The World's Fair Hotel would become known as "The Murder Castle."

The Murder Castle, designed by Dr. H. H. Holmes contained a creatively odd labyrinth of windowless rooms, pointless stairwells, and torture chambers. By today's standards, that's just another boutique hotel in New York's Hell's Kitchen. What gave Murder Castle its legacy was H. H. Holmes, who designed it as some sort of demented body part factory.

Dr. Holmes, born Herman Webster Mudgett, has the illustrious honor of being the United States' first documented serial killer. He was also a medically trained pharmacist who had enough knowledge to dissect and skin his victims and sell their parts to hospitals and training facilities.

Holmes, in his Murder Castle created soundproof rooms, equipped with sealed windows to enable himself to asphyxiate his victims by gas. The bodies were then transported easily into the preparation area by way of a web of secret chutes built into the structure of the hotel. The body would slide down an elaborate chute and arrive onto a pile of other bodies. From there H.H. Holmes would dissect and skin the bodies, prepping the body parts for resale. Some bodies he would cremate and others he would put into a pit of acid.

Holmes, not only created a lucrative business of selling body parts but also streamlined the process of killing, dissecting and disposing of the bodies, making it into something that Henry Ford would have envied.

All in all, Dr. H. H. Holmes was just a natural-born capitalist… a twisted, demented and highly disturbed capitalist. But a capitalist nonetheless.

Holmes later traveled throughout the United States, scheming his way from state-to-state. It all eventually caught up to him after Holmes was incarcerated for running an insurance scam.

It's estimated that H. H. Holmes murdered up to 200 people during a six-year span in the late 1800s.

He was hanged.

March 1

"I want to master life and death."

Name: Ted Bundy
Killings: 30-36+
Location: United States (scattered)
Years active: 1969 (possibly as early as 1961) - 1978
Fun Fact: Signed Christmas cards Bundy sent out a month or so
before his execution are worth thousands of dollars at auction.

March 2

"The whore will suffer more than she has ever done so tonight, that thought revitalizes me."

(no pic available)

Name: Jack the Ripper
Nickname: Jack the Ripper
Killings: 5+
Location: England
Years active: 1888-1891
Fun Fact: Because of how cleanly organs were removed, many thought Jack might be a doctor.

March 3

"I just wondered how it would feel to shoot Grandma."

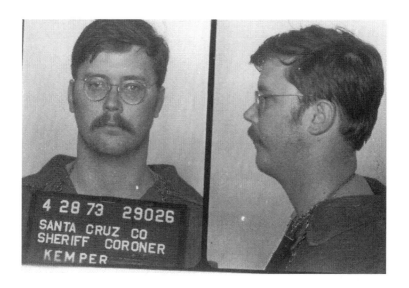

Name: Ed Kemper
Nickname: The Co-Ed Killer
Killings: 10
Location: California
Years active: 1964-1973
Fun Fact: Kemper told a judge he should be tortured to death.

March 4

"I thought of myself causing accidents affecting thousands of people and invented a number of crazy fantasies such as smashing bridges and boring through bridge piers."

Name: Peter Kurten
Nickname: The Dusseldorf Vampire
Killings: 9-60
Location: Germany
Years active: 1913-1929
Fun Fact: Kurten was studied by celebrated psychologist Karl Berg.

March 5

"These are bloodythirsty times."

Name: Richard Ramirez
Nickname: The Night Stalker
Killings: 14
Location: California
Years active: 1984-1985
Fun Fact: Ramirez was married in prison. His wife wore a silver
wedding band as Satanists don't wear gold.

March 6

"Ain't no way I'm homosexual, I have no grudge against [homosexuals] as long as they keep their hands to themselves. I'm scared."

Name: Wayne Bertram Williams
Nickname: The Atlanta Child Killer; The Atlanta Monster; The Atlanta Child Murderer
Killings: 2-31
Location: Georgia
Years active: 1979-1981
Fun Fact: Williams was known as a liar who was once arrested for impersonating a police officer.

March 7

"I stood my ground to earn respect. I'm no woman killer, and I am angry as hell and will fight for my honor to exist."

Name: Randy Woodfield
Nickname: The I-5 Killer
Killings: 18
Location: California, Oregon
Years active: 1979-1981
Fun Fact: Woodfield was drafted by the Green Bay Packers despite numerous arrests for public indecency.

March 8

"Me-37; SFPD-0."

Name: Zodiac Killer
Nickname: Zodiac Killer
Killings: 5-28
Location: California
Years active: 1960s-1970s
Fun Fact: There have been numerous suspects in this case but no one has ever been caught. Check out some suspects here: http://www.zodiackiller.com/Suspects.html

March 9

"I love Stateville. This is my home."

(speaking about life in prison, where he somehow gained access to illegal drugs like cocaine, and had frequent sex with other inmates)

Name: Richard Speck
Nickname/AKA: Richard Lindberg
Killings: 8
Location: Illinois
Years active: 1966
Fun Fact: Speck had a tattoo that said "Born to Raise Hell"

March 10

"I am the fellow who goes around doing people good. I put people out of their misery."

Name: Carl Panzram
Nickname/AKA: Jefferson Davis
Killings: 22
Location: United States (scattered)
Years active: 1915-1929
Fun Fact: Panzram claimed he would rape men not because he was homosexual, but because it was his way of dominating and humiliating them.

March 11

"It was my morality and sense of justice which revealed all."

Name: Dennis Nilsen
Nickname: The Kindly Killer
Killings: 15
Location: England
Years active: 1978-1983
Fun Fact: Nilsen was called the Kindly Killer because he felt his method of murder, strangulation or drowning, was humane.

March 12

"A rock doesn't make a decision while it's falling. It just falls."

Name: Herbert Mullin
Killings: 13
Location: California
Years active: 1972-1973
Fun Fact: Mullins's father was a WWII war hero.

March 13

"Maybe I should kill you to show you that there's no such thing as death."

Name: Charles Manson
Killings: 5
Location: California
Years active: 1969
Fun Fact: Manson never killed anyone himself. He commanded his followers to do it.

March 14

"Just to put them out of their misery, and, besides, they really are a nuisance to everyone around them. Take the first one I killed, for instance. Christian Hitgers, I mean. I had to change his bedclothes several times a day and I got tired of it. So I said to Hitgers: I'm not going to change any more bed clothes for you. I gave him a glass of beer which contained arsenic."

Name: Frederick Mors
Nickname: Herr Doktor
Killings: 8
Location: New York
Years active: 1914-1915
Fun Fact: While not actually a doctor, Mors often wore a lab coat with a stethoscope.

March 15

"We strangled them by hand. We strangled them by rope. We even stabbed them when we strangled them. We even tied them so they would strangle themselves."

Name: Henry Lee Lucas
Nickname: The Confession Killer
Killings: 3+
Location: United States (scattered)
Years active: 1960-1983
Fun Fact: After he was arrested, Lucas originally claimed he had killed 500 people.

March 16

"I ripped her clothes off her, ripped off her slip, and put it around her neck, then the stockings... Whew! So tight."

Name: Albert DeSalvo
Nickname: The Boston Strangler
Killings: 13
Location: Boston, MA
Years active: 1962-1964
Fun Fact: DeSalvo would pose the bodies of his victims.

March 17

"They are more like us than we like to admit. I had these excessive desires and thoughts, wanting to control them."

Name: Jeffrey Dahmer
Nickname: The Milwaukee Cannibal; The Milwaukee Monster
Killings: 17
Location: Wisconsin
Years active: 1978-1991
Fun Fact: Dahmer kept numerous body parts in his small apartment as trophies.

March 18

"She was a hooker. Angelo went and picked her up. I was waiting in the street. He drove around to where I was. I got in the car. We got on the freeway. I fucked and killed her. We dumped the body off and that was it. Nothing to it."

Name: Kenneth Bianchi
Nickname: The Hillside Strangler(s) (with his cousin Angelo Buono)
Killings: 12
Location: California, Washington
Years active: 1977-1979
Fun Fact: When caught, Bianchi pretended that he had multiple personalities and that it was "Billy" that committed the murders.

March 19

"They dress and paint up and give you the come-on, and you can't help thinking that they wouldn't look nearly so cheeky or so saucy if they were helpless or dead."

Name: John Christie
Nickname: The Rillington Place Strangler
Killings: 8
Location: England
Years active: 1943-1953
Fun Fact: Christie was a postman who was sent to prison for stealing postal orders.

March 20

**"Even I could not understand it. I think I must have
had a kind of magnetism. They followed me like dogs."**
(Commenting on why his victims followed him to their bloody doom)

Name: Andrei Chikatilo
Nickname: The Butcher of Rostov; The Red Ripper; The Forest Strip
Killer; The Rostov Ripper
Killings: 53-56+
Location: Russia
Years active: 1978-1990
Fun Fact: Chikatilo claimed he could only achieve sexual arousal
from stabbing and slashing women.

March 21

"Self protection required that the girl be killed."

Name: Ted Bundy
Killings: 30-36+
Location: United States (scattered)
Years active: 1969 (possibly as early as 1961) - 1978
Fun Fact: Bundy was an honor student at the University of Washington.

March 22

"After the first one, I couldn't do anything about it. He (Bonin) had a hypnotic way about him."

(Talking about his partner William Bonin)

Name: Vernon Butts
Nickname: The Freeway Strangler
Killings: 36
Location: California
Years active: 1979-1980
Fun Fact: Butts killed himself while awaiting trial.

March 23

"They were no good, they deserved to die. It had to be done. But I only killed a couple of them. I ain't worried. My cousin's gonna go into his little nut bag."

Name: Angelo Buono
Nickname: The Hillside Strangler(s) (with his cousin Kenneth Bianchi)
Killings: 10
Location: California
Years active: 1977-1978
Fun Fact: Buono made women refer to him as the "Italian Stallion."

March 24

"I wanted them to be a part of me - and now they are."

(Talking about cutting the flesh from two of his victims' legs and then cooking it in a macaroni casserole)

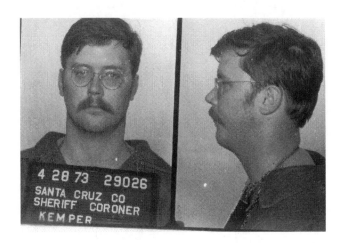

Name: Ed Kemper
Nickname: The Co-Ed Killer
Killings: 10
Location: California
Years active: 1964-1973
Fun Fact: As a child Kemper would mutilate his sister's dolls.

March 25

"I think what has to be done is not to try and convince or persuade the majority of people that we are right, as much as try to increase tensions in society to the point where things start to break down. So the question is how do you increase those tensions?"

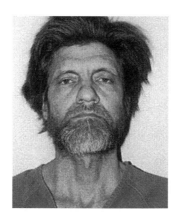

Name: Theodore Kaczynski
Nickname: The Unabomber
Killings: 3 killed, dozens attempted
Location: United States (scattered)
Years active: 1978-1995
Fun Fact: Kaczynski's murders were his attempt to save the human race from becoming enslaved by technology. He only bombed people involved in the high-tech industry. Among other things, he believes that artifical intelligence will one day become smarter than humanity, and that nanobots (microscopic robots) could run amok and wipe out all life on earth.

March 26

"All I need is a plastic toothpick. I put this in and the door opened."

Name: Albert DeSalvo
Nickname: The Boston Strangler
Killings: 13
Location: Boston, MA
Years active: 1962-1964
Fun Fact: A Texas legislator honored DeSalvo for "population control" as an April Fool's joke.

March 27

"I knew it was just a matter of time. I'm glad it's over."

(Talking about getting caught)

Name: Gregory Clepper
Nickname: The South Side Strangler
Killings: 8+
Location: Chicago
Years active: 1991-1996
Fun Fact: Clepper's mother helped him dispose of at least one body.

March 28

"If you want to say I slept in the same house with a dead body, OK, fine. I'll buy that - but in the same room, no! And besides, the dead won't bother you - it's the living you've got to worry about."

Name: John Wayne Gacy
Nickname: The Killer Clown
Killings: 34
Location: Illinois
Years active: 1972-1978
Fun Fact: His last words were "Kiss My Ass."

March 29

"Honestly, her last words were 'I can't breathe.' I still puzzle over the post mortem dismemberment and cutting. There must be something deep in my subconscious that really needs that kind of macabre action."

Name: Sean Vincent Gillis
Killings: 8
Location: Louisiana
Years active: 1994-2004
Fun Fact: Gillis said he waited a long time between kills because he was "happy."

March 30

"Look at this useless thing. What do you think I could do with that? I am not a homosexual... I have milk in my breasts. I am going to give birth!"

Name: Andrei Chikatilo
Nickname: The Butcher of Rostov; The Red Ripper; The Forest Strip Killer; The Rostov Ripper
Killings: 53-56+
Location: Russia
Years active: 1978-1990
Fun Fact: During his trial the judge would often tell Chikatilo, "Shut your mouth."

"I am Christ!"

Name: Albert Fish
Nickname/AKA: Thomas Frank Howard
Killings: 10+
Location: New York
Years active: 1924-1932
Fun Fact: Fish would often insert needles into his scrotum.

April

April's featured Serial Killer is: Carl Panzram

They just don't make 'em anymore like they made Carl Panzram; he was one of the most unrepentant and misanthropic characters in the history of serial killers. He truly had no moral compass and, because of that, the world endured his brand of evil from Panzram's pre-teen years on a Minnesota farm through his adulthood.

Panzram's pure repulsive personality can rival any Bond villain: cold, heartless, without remorse and with a devilishly evil plan. In his autobiography Panzram devised a plan to start a war between Britain and the United States; he expected to profit from stocks that he imagined would skyrocket from a war between the countries. Bond villain? Sure sounds like it.

Kind of like Haliburton, if Haliburton was only one guy.

Panzram didn't want just want to kill you; he wanted to rip your still beating heart from your warm body, and hold it in front of your eyes while he sodomized and tortured you. Ultimately it would end by either the victim being beaten by Panzram's bare hands or being shot by a stolen gun.

Hugely strong, he claimed to have raped and sodomized over 1000 men and children. He didn't sodomize them for fun though, Hell no. He claimed that he derived no sexual pleasure from raping the men but rather he wanted to dominate and humiliate them.

He was known to have committed 22 murders but with the rage and hatred he had for humans, some suggest that number was the smallest possible number of victims.

While in prison, Panzram wrote his autobiography, which told the story of a warped child that had no chance of a normal life. From his own words he described the twisted journey that led him to his final prison cell, then to the end of a rope.

At his hanging, when Panzram was asked if he had any last words, he said: "Hurry up you Hoosier bastard, I could kill ten men while you're fooling around."

His body is interned at the United States Penitentiary Cemetery in Leavenworth.

April 1

"I just enjoyed killin' them."

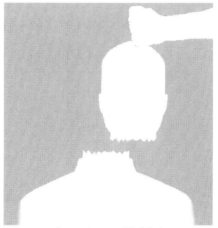

(no pic available)

Name: Joe Fischer
Nickname: "Crazy" Joe Fischer
Killings: 2-40+
Location: United States (scattered), possibly China
Years active: 1959-1979
Fun Fact: Fischer claimed he killed well over 100 people.

April 2

"She was from way the hell up north in Minnesota. I asked her if she came to North Carolina to get warm, and she said she had run away from home because her hateful step-daddy was always doing things to her, which I took to mean he raped her, and I said I sure understood all about hating step-daddies."

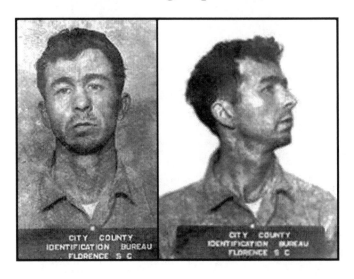

Name: Donald Gaskins
Nickname: Pee Wee
Killings: 10-110+
Location: South Carolina, North Carolina, Georgia, Florida
Years active: 1953-1982
Fun Fact: Gaskins was teased and called "Pee Wee" as a child. His childhood was so neglectful that he apparently didn't know his real name until the first time he was arrested.

April 3

"It might have been thirty. It might have been forty. I don't remember."

(When asked how many boys he had killed)

Name: Friedrich "Fritz" Haarman
Nickname: The Butcher of Hanover; The Wolf Man; The Vampire of Hanover
Killings: 24-27+
Location: Germany
Years active: 1918-1924
Fun Fact: Rumor has it that Haarman would sell meat from his victims as black market pork.

April 4

"I'll write my own story."

(About his aspirations of being a writer).

Name: Robert Hansen
Killings: 17-21+
Location: Alaska
Years active: 1971–1983
Fun Fact: An Alaskan pilot, he was known for sadistically stalking his prey, normally naked prostitutes, throughout the secluded Alaskan woods.

April 5

"If I ever get caught, I'm going to act crazy. I'm going to go into court and salute everybody."

Name: Gary Heidnik
Nickname: Brother Bishop
Killings: 2+
Location: Philadelphia
Years active: 1986-1987
Fun Fact: Heidnik kept numerous women captive in his basement, although he only killed 2.

April 6

"This is what Bell County has done to me! I hope all this is worth it, Texas!"

Name: George Jo Hennard
Killings: 23
Location: Texas
Years active: 1991
Fun Fact: Hennard was known for keeping his lawn very well manicured.

April 7

"I killed thousands in Vietnam, and I want to kill more!"

Name: James Oliver Huberty
Nickname: San Ysidro Massacre Killer
Killings: 21
Location: California
Years active: 1984
Fun Fact: The day before the massacre Huberty called a mental health center. His name was written down as "Shouberty." Huberty never served in any branch of the armed forces.

April 8

"Blood was an actual pain in the ass."

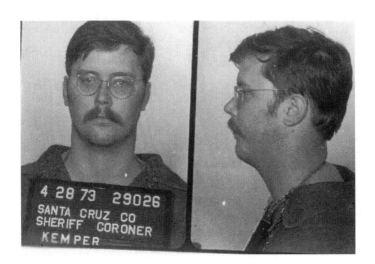

Name: Ed Kemper
Nickname: The Co-Ed Killer
Killings: 10
Location: California
Years active: 1964-1973
Fun Fact: After killing one innocent girl named Aiko Koo, Ed drove around town with her body in the trunk of his car. He dismembered her body and had sex with her corpse and buried the parts in a shallow ditch. The very next day, as part of conditions of his parole, Ed drove, in the same car, still seeping with the bloody remnants of Aiko in his trunk, to meet with a court appointed group of psychiatrists. Ed was, if anything, punctual.

April 9

"I have no remorse. As to whether recollection of my deeds makes me feel ashamed, I will tell you. Thinking back to all the details is not at all unpleasant. I rather enjoy it."

Name: Peter Kurten
Nickname: The Dusseldorf Vampire
Killings: 9-60
Location: Germany
Years active: 1913-1929
Fun Fact: Kurten's father was jailed for having sex with Kurten's 13 year old sister.

April 10

"I am very sorry, but I must not keep these gentlemen waiting."

(On his way to the guillotine)

Name: Henri Desire Landru
Nickname: The Bluebeard of Gambais
Killings: 11
Location: France
Years active: 1915-1919
Fun Fact: Landru would burn his victims' bodies in his oven.

April 11

"Take your worst nightmares, and put my face to them."

Name: Tommy Lynn Sells
Nickname: The Cross Country Killer
Killings: 22+
Location: United States (scattered)
Years active: 1980-1999
Fun Fact: Sells claims he committed his first murder when he was 16.

April 12

"I put the head into a pot, popped the lid on and lit the stove. Later I listened to music and had a good drink, also watching some TV as the head was simmering."

Name: Dennis Nilsen
Nickname: The Kindly Killer
Killings: 15
Location: England
Years active: 1978-1983
Fun Fact: Nilsen had a sexual relationship in prison with David Martin, who was a UK Bank robber, well known for cross dressing.

April 13

"I thought you would come yesterday... I liked the boys and I didn't want them to go to hell."

(Speaking to the policemen who arrested him)

Name: Marcelo Costa de Andrade
Nickname: The Vampire of Niterói
Killings: 14
Location: Brazil
Years active: 1991
Fun Fact: When 17 he attempted to rape his 10 year old brother.

April 14

"I'm going to make you feel better."

Name: Richard Angelo
Nickname: The Good Samaritan Killer
Killings: 8
Location: New York
Years active: 1987
Fun Fact: Angelo was an Eagle Scout and a volunteer fireman.

April 15

"I realized these girls were just little girls like mine.... I started to understand just how much it would hurt to have someone do what I had done."

Name: Roberto Arguelles
Killings: 4+
Location: Utah
Years active: 1992-1997
Fun Fact: In court Arguelles was strapped in a wheelchair and had on a mask to protect officers.

April 16

"She kept begging and pleading and pleading and begging, and I got sick of listening to her, so I stabbed her."

(Speaking about Sharon Tate)

Name: Susan Atkins
Nickname/AKA: Sadie Mae Glutz
Killings: 5
Location: California
Years active: 1969
Fun Fact: Atkins was denied parole 18 times.

April 17

"Fuck off, we murder, watch out, Fanny and Faggot."

(Scribbled on the wall of a nursery)

Name: Mary Bell
Nickname: The Tyneside Strangler
Killings: 2+
Location: England
Years active: 1968
Fun Fact: Bell was 11 years old when she committed her murders, making her the youngest known serial killer. She was released from prison when she was 23 and has been living anonymously ever since. She is now a grandmother.

April 18

"I am a monster. I am the Son of Sam and love to hunt."

(From a letter at a crime scene)

Name: David Berkowitz
Nickname: The Son of Sam
Killings: 6
Location: New York City
Years active: 1976-1977
Fun Fact: The Son of Sam law is designed to keep criminals from profiting from their crimes.

April 19

"I'm glad you caught me, because I'd do it again."

Name: Arthur Bishop
Nickname: Eagle Scout Killer
Killings: 5
Location: Utah
Years active: 1979-1983
Fun Fact: Bishop blamed pornography for his murdering young boys.

April 20

"They say it's the number of people I killed. I say it's the principle."

Name: Aileen Wuornos
Killings: 7
Location: Florida
Years active: 1989-1990
Fun Fact: Wournos claimed all of her victims raped or attempted to rape her and all her acts were in self defense.

April 21

"My morals and constitutional rights has been broken. I ain't taking any procedure in the trial."

Name: Angelo Buono
Nickname: The Hillside Strangler(s)
Killings: 10
Location: California
Years active: 1977-1978
Fun Fact: Buono and his cousin, Kenneth Bianchi, would show most victims fake police badges to lure them into their vehicle.

April 22

"I'm in charge of the entertainment."

Name: Ted Bundy
Killings: 30-36+
Location: United States (scattered)
Years active: 1969 (possibly as early as 1961) - 1978
Fun Fact: Bundy's first serious girlfriend was a practical woman
and seemed to realize that Ted had some serious character flaws that
took him out of the running as "husband material."

April 23

"I always thought about this, and suffered because I realized that I was different from everyone else."

(Talking about his sexual urges)

Name: Andrei Chikatilo
Nickname: The Butcher of Rostov; The Red Ripper; The Forest Strip Killer; The Rostov Ripper
Killings: 53-56+
Location: Russia
Years active: 1978-1990
Fun Fact: Chikatilo was so brutal that when bodies were found some locals feared it was the act of werewolves.

April 24

"I regret with all my heart what my hand has done. I have taken what I cannot return. If only I could bend back the hands of that ageless clock and change the past. Ah, but alas, I am not the keeper of time, only a small part of history and the legacy of man's fall from grace. I'm sorry."

Name: Danny Rolling
Nickname: The Gainesville Ripper
Killings: 8
Location: Florida
Years active: 1989-1990
Fun Fact: Final meal: Lobster tail, shrimp, a baked potato, strawberry cheese cake and sweet tea.

April 25

"I'm going to introduce you to my friends down there."

Name: Gary Heidnik
Nickname: Brother Bishop
Killings: 2+
Location: Philadelphia
Years active: 1986-1987
Fun Fact: Heidnik started the "United Church of the Ministers of God." He was its only ordained minister. There was over $500,000 in the church account when he was arrested.

April 26

"I will take the first whore I encounter and show her what hell is really like... My head aches."

(no pic available)

Name: Jack the Ripper
Nickname: The Whitechapel Murderer
Killings: 5+
Location: England
Years active: 1888-1891
Fun Fact: There are numerous Jack the Ripper tours in the U.K.

April 27

"I'm not going to hurt you. I'm only going to tie you up. I need your money to go to New Orleans."

Name: Richard Speck
Nickname/AKA: Richard Lindberg
Killings: 8
Location: Illinois
Years active: 1966
Fun Fact: One can find a video of Speck in prison in which he does cocaine and performs oral sex on another inmate. He also appears to have breasts as a result of taking hormones.

April 28

"I have done it again."

(no pic available)

Name: Lucian Staniak
Nickname: The Red Spider
Killings: 6-20
Location: Poland
Years active: 1964-1967
Fun Fact: Police grew suspicious of Staniak when they broke into his locker and found a painting of a disemboweled woman with flowers growing out of her stomach.

April 29

"Hell, no! No one ever did anything for me! Why the hell should I do anything for anyone else?"

(On the suggestion that he donate his eyes for transplant)

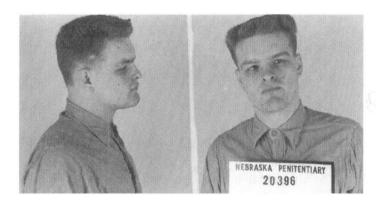

Name: Charles Starkweather
Nickname: Badlands Killer
Killings: 11
Location: Wyoming, Nebraska
Years active: 1957-1958
Fun Fact: Starkweather was fixated on James Dean, and mimicked his appearance and persona.

April 30

"Bates had to die, there will be more."

(Letter addressed to the Riverside Police Department, April 30, 1967)

Name: Zodiac Killer
Nickname: Zodiac Killer
Killings: 5-28
Location: California
Years active: 1960s-1970s
Fun Fact: On November 8, 1969, the Zodiac mailed a card to the San Francisco Chronicle with a cryptogram consisting of 340 characters. The 340-character cipher has never been decoded.

May

May's featured serial killer is Ted Bundy.

Poor Ted, he never really had a chance. But then again, neither did any of his victims.

Ted Bundy, born to a single mom, was brought up thinking that his mom was not his mom. Rather, he was told that his grandparents were his parents and that his mom, who was in her mid-to-late twenties by then, was Bundy's older sister.

Bundy hated women and it was thought that his hatred began because he felt that he was betrayed by two important women in his life, his mother and his first love.

Sure, when you find out that your sister is really your mom, that has got to be jolting. But when his first love broke up with Bundy because she felt there wasn't a future between the two of them, Bundy took it hard.

Following the ugly breakup from his girlfriend he sought refuge in one thought: revenge. As with many broken hearted individuals, they find an outlet, a mission. His mission was to break her heart and then go on a murdering spree, killing anyone that looked remotely like his first love.

Bundy and his trail of 35 small-framed, female bodies became one of the biggest stories and most notable serial killers of modern times. He was a woman's worst nightmare. He was charismatic. He was clean cut. He was well-spoken and when he spoke with you, he would look into your eyes and smile to rope you in for the kill. If it weren't for the fact that he was an egomaniac, he may have gone on for many more years.

He could attract women like flies at a barbeque. He knew how to manipulate and prey on women by understanding their compassionate nature. Bundy was known for pretending to be injured or in need of some help. And when an unsuspecting female would assist this injured guy, it never ended well. Sooner or later, she was stuffed into the car, gagged, raped then murdered. For some women, he would rape them after they were dead.

Other times he cut right to the chase and would sneak into the victim's room and bludgeon them.

Bundy was also known to be the type of serial killer to keep trinkets or mementos from the victims. He would have keepsakes, and liked taking Polaroid pictures and posing with the victims. He liked to keep the photos close by so he wouldn't forget the moment.

Bundy confessed to killing 30 women. However in multiple other reports, from interviews and published reports, the number is quite higher. In an exchange with an FBI agent, where the agents suggested 36 as the number of murdered women, Bundy replied: "Add one digit to that and you'll have it."

Bundy was executed by electric chair in 1982.

May 1

"For what reason I don't know, I stuck the bottle in her."

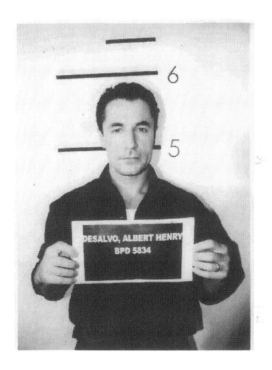

Name: Albert DeSalvo
Nickname: The Boston Strangler
Killings: 13
Location: Boston, MA
Years active: 1962-1964
Fun Fact: DeSalvo was stabbed to death in a prison infirmary. No one was ever convicted for his murder.

May 2

"Fuck you! Power to the people!"

Name: Mark Essex
Killings: 9
Location: New Orleans, LA
Years active: 1972-1973
Fun Fact: Essex's apartment was covered from floor to ceiling with anti-white graffiti.

May 3

"I carried it too far, that's for sure."

Name: Jeffrey Dahmer
Nickname: The Milwaukee Cannibal; The Milwaukee Monster
Killings: 17
Location: Wisconsin
Years active: 1978-1991
Fun Fact: The novel "Zombie" by Joyce Carol Oates is a fictional rendition of Dahmer's life and crimes.

May 4

"My second murder was a really clever murder. Much, much cleverer than the first one."

Name: John Christie
Nickname: The Rillington Place Strangler
Killings: 8
Location: England
Years active: 1943-1953
Fun Fact: Christie gave a victim a homemade inhaler filled with perfumed water – and something more. He modified the inhaler by running a tube in the device to a gas outlet. After the victim became dazed, he tied her up, raped and strangled her, then buried her in his garden.

May 5

"I will in all probability be convicted, but I will not go away as a monster, but as a tragedy."

(no pic available)

Name: Joel Rifkin
Killings: 9-17+
Location: New York
Years active: 1974-1991
Fun Fact: Rifkin was captured after he kidnapped and murdered the girlfriend of Dave Rubinstein, singer for 1980s punk rock band Reagan Youth. Rubinstein was a drug addict whose girlfriend Tiffany Bresciani, was a prostitute. Rubinstein saw Bresciani get into Rifkin's pickup truck, and gave police its description.

May 6

"I told them before I ever left prison that I was going to commit crimes, told them the type of crimes I was going to commit, and they wouldn't believe it. They said I was going regardless of whether I liked it or not. And the day I got out of jail is the day I started killing."

Name: Henry Lee Lucas
Nickname: The Confession Killer
Killings: 3+
Location: United States (scattered)
Years active: 1960-1983
Fun Fact: While there is no doubt Lucas killed numerous people, in some circles he is known as a huge liar because of the sheer number of killings he claimed.

May 7

"I said she's gotta die and I've gotta die, or girls like that are gonna die. And that's when I decided to murder my mother."

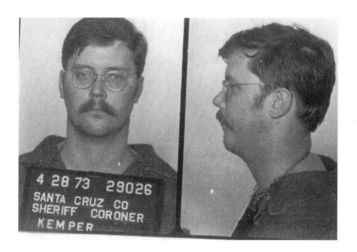

Name: Ed Kemper
Nickname: The Co-Ed Killer
Killings: 10
Location: California
Years active: 1964-1973
Fun Fact: When Kemper was growing up he imagined killing everyone in town and having sex with all the corpses.

May 8

"The first person I killed was sort of an accident. The second time, the people had made a lot of money and I was jealous. I was being watched, and I shot this lady - got some blood out of it. I went to another house, walked in, a whole family was there. I shot the whole family. Somebody saw me there. I saw this girl. She had called the police and they had been unable to locate me. Curt Silva's girlfriend - he was killed in a motorcycle accident, and I had this idea that he was killed through the syndicate, that he was in the Mafia. The whole syndicate was making money by having my mom poison me."

Name: Richard Chase
Nickname: The Dracula Killer; The Vampire of Sacramento; The Vampire Killer
Killings: 6
Location: California
Years active: 1977-1978
Fun Fact: Chase drank the blood of his victims and ate their internal organs. He did this because of a delusion involving making sure Nazis didn't turn his blood into powder.

May 9

"They deserved to die."

Name: Ilfreide Blauensteiner
Nickname: The Black Widow
Killings: 3+
Location: Austria
Years active: 1981-1995
Fun Fact: Many feel that she killed because she needed money to
fuel a gambling addiction.

May 10

"I was a greedy, ravenous individual, hungry for life, determined to rise from the bottom... it wasn't me!"

Name: Jack Unterweger
Nickname: Jack the Writer
Killings: 10+
Location: Austria, California
Years active: 1974-1992
Fun Fact: Unterweger was released in 1990 for a 1974 murder. Before he started killing again, Unterweger was considered a poster boy for rehabilitation.

May 11

"It was slick and I brought my hand to my face and I could smell the blood. I opened my mouth and licked it on my fingers..."

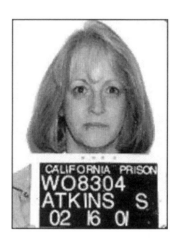

Name: Susan Atkins
Nickname/AKA: Sadie Mae Glutz; member of the Manson Family
Killings: 5
Location: California
Years active: 1969
Fun Fact: You can read about Susan Atkins's Bible studies here:
http://www.susanatkins.org/02-BibleStudies.html

May 12

"It was just like it should be. You shot them, and they fell."

Name: David Berkowitz
Nickname: The Son of Sam
Killings: 6
Location: New York City
Years active: 1976-1977
Fun Fact: When Berkowitz wrote a letter to New York Daily News columnist Jimmy Breslin, the paper printed some of it. 1.1 million copies of the paper were sold that day.

May 13

"I don't feel guilty for anything. I feel sorry for people who feel guilt."

Name: Ted Bundy
Killings: 30-36+
Location: United States (scattered)
Years active: 1969 (possibly as early as 1961) - 1978
Fun Fact: Young Ted was active in the Methodist Church and even served as Vice President of the Methodist Youth Fellowship.

May 14

"The purpose of life is to leave your mark on this earth."

(Speaking about why he killed.)

Name: Andrei Chikatilo
Nickname: The Butcher of Rostov; The Red Ripper; The Forest Strip
Killer; The Rostov Ripper
Killings: 53-56+
Location: Russia
Years active: 1978-1990
Fun Fact: Chikatilo was kept in a cage during his trial.

May 15

"I feel it's wrong for people who commit crimes to try to shift the blame to someone else, onto their parents, or onto their upbringing or living circumstances. I think that's just a cop-out. I take full responsibility."

Name: Jeffrey Dahmer
Nickname: The Milwaukee Cannibal; The Milwaukee Monster
Killings: 17
Location: Wisconsin
Years active: 1978-1991
Fun Fact: In high school a group of Dahmer's acquaintances formed the "Jeffrey Dahmer Fan Club."

May 16

"Attractiveness had nothing to do with it... When this certain time comes on me, it's a very immediate thing. When I get this feeling, instead of going to work I make an excuse to my boss. I start driving and I start building this image up, and that's why I find myself not knowing where I'm going."

Name: Albert DeSalvo
Nickname: The Boston Strangler
Killings: 13
Location: Boston, MA
Years active: 1962-1964
Fun Fact: DeSalvo was incarcerated for a series of rapes. He was known for saying, "I'm sorry," when leaving the apartment of his victims.

May 17

"I'll let my lawyers talk for me. I'm ready to go."

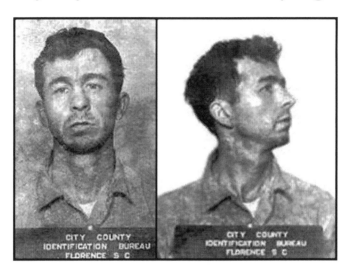

Name: Donald Gaskins
Nickname: Pee Wee
Killings: 10-110+
Location: South Carolina, North Carolina, Georgia, Florida
Years active: 1953-1982
Fun Fact: Gaskins claimed to have killed over 100 people.

May 18

"If the law won't kill me, I shall kill myself. I fully realize that I am not fit to live among people in a civilized community. I have no desire to do so."

Name: Carl Panzram
Nickname/AKA: Jefferson Davis
Killings: 22
Location: United States (scattered)
Years active: 1915-1929
Fun Fact: At one point Panzram bought a yacht with stolen money. Over time he lured ten different sailors on board with the promise of free liquor. He got them drunk, raped all of them, shot them, and dumped them in the ocean.

May 19

"I would have gone on and on. It was like some sort of drug."

Name: Peter Sutcliffe
Nickname: The Yorkshire Ripper
Killings: 13
Location: England
Years active: 1975-1980
Fun Fact: While in prison, Sutcliffe lost his left eye after being stabbed with a pen in 1997.

May 20

"When we took 'em out and cut 'em up... remember one time I said I wanted me some ribs? Did that make me a cannibal?"

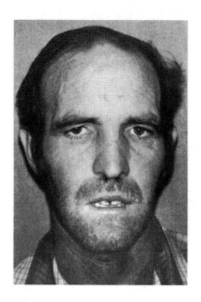

Name: Ottis Toole
Killings: 6+
Location: Florida
Years active: 1975-1983
Fun Fact: Toole confessed to the murder of the son of John Walsh, host of "Americas Most Wanted."

May 21

"Miss Bates was stupid. She went to the slaughter like a lamb. She did not put up a struggle. But I did. It was a ball."

Name: Zodiac Killer
Nickname: Zodiac Killer
Killings: 5-28
Location: California
Years active: 1960s-1970s
Fun Fact: The last letter from the Zodiac Killer was received in 1974.

May 22

"I may have told many lies, and I may have played many games."

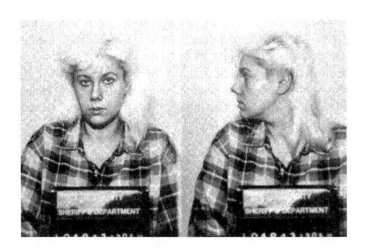

Name: Cathy Wood
Nickname: The Lethal Lovers
Killings: 5
Location: Michigan
Years active: 1987
Fun Fact: Wood and her lesbian lover were nurse's aides who killed elderly women for a sexual thrill. The original idea was to spell out "MURDER" with the victims names.

May 23

"Life is not worth living."

Name: Charles Whitman
Nickname: The Texas Tower Sniper
Killings: 16
Location: Austin, Texas
Years active: 1966
Fun Fact: Whitman was a marine who was court-martialed for gambling.

May 24

"I'm the devil. I'm here to do the devil's business."

Name: Charles Watson
Nickname: "Tex" Watson
Killings: 5
Location: California
Years active: 1969
Fun Fact: Tex Watson was a member of the Manson Family. He now runs http://www.aboundinglove.org/

May 25

"This world is nothing but evil, and my own evil just happened to come out cause of the circumstances of what I was doing."

Name: Aileen Wuornos
Killings: 7
Location: Florida
Years active: 1989-1990
Fun Fact: Wournos scored 32 out of 40 on a test to assess whether she was a psychopath.

May 26

"It was supposed to be my way out, the last fling before the ending. Guess it's better than just going out like a light with no flicker."

Name: Charles Starkweather
Nickname: Badlands Killer
Killings: 11
Location: Wyoming, Nebraska
Years active: 1957-1958
Fun Fact: Billy Joel namechecks the Starkweather murders in his song "We Didn't Start the Fire."

May 27

"I picked a juicy flower in Olsztyn and I shall do it again somewhere else, for there is no holiday without a funeral."

(no pic available)

Name: Lucian Staniak
Nickname: The Red Spider
Killings: 6-20
Location: Poland
Years active: 1964-1967
Fun Fact: Staniak was known as the "Red Spider" because he sent anonymous letters to either newspapers or the police, warning them that he was going to commit murder, written in spidery, red handwriting.

May 28

"I like children... they're tasty."

Name: Albert Fish
Nickname/AKA: Thomas Frank Howard
Killings: 10+
Location: New York
Years active: 1924-1932
Fun Fact: Fish is suspected of also being the "Brooklyn Vampire," a rapist and murderer that preyed on children.

May 29

"Widower with children, aged forty-three, with comfortable income, affectionate, serious and moving in good society, desires to meet widow with a view of matrimony."

(Classified ad)

Name: Henri Desire Landru
Nickname: The Bluebeard of Gambais
Killings: 11
Location: France
Years active: 1915-1919
Fun Fact: His aliases were so numerous that he had to keep a ledger listing all the women with whom he corresponded and which particular identity he used for each woman.

May 30

"I derived no sexual satisfaction from what I did. My motives were principally to arouse excitement and indignation in the population. Through setting fire to the body I thought I would increase the rage."

Name: Peter Kurten
Nickname: The Dusseldorf Vampire
Killings: 9-60
Location: Germany
Years active: 1913-1929
Fun Fact: His last meal was Wienerschnitzel, fried potatoes, and a bottle of white wine.

May 31

"As I was growing up I shied away from loud noises and arguments."

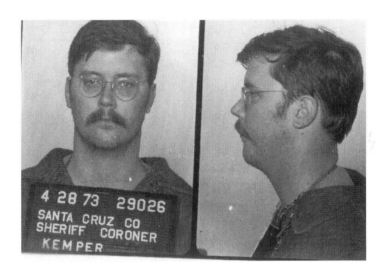

Name: Ed Kemper
Nickname: The Co-Ed Killer
Killings: 10
Location: California
Years active: 1964-1973
Fun Fact: When Kemper called the police to confess they initially didn't believe him.

June

June's featured serial killer is John Wayne Gacy.

Born March 17, 1942, in Chicago, Illinois, John Wayne Gacy lived through an abusive childhood at the hands of his parents and a long-term struggle over his own sexuality.

Gacy, like many serial killers, survived an awful childhood. With a verbally and physically abusive father, Gacy sought refuge wherever he could find it. But sometimes when you are seven, you are the victim of those around you; Gacy was molested by a family friend who would take Gacy for rides in his truck and fondle him. Gacy had nowhere to hide.

As an adult, he was a man that hid everything about himself and fought his own demons. Questioning his own sexuality at a time when being homosexual was akin to a disease, Gacy hid his sexual urges. But those urges would manifest themselves in an awkward and devious manner.

He tried to assimilate into society. He did all the things that society expected. He met a woman and got married. He had a family... bought a house.... had a good stable job... he molested underage boys.

After being convicted of sexual assault in 1968, his life went into a downward spiral. But after his wife divorced him and he spent 18 months in jail, in 1970, he emerged a changed man. Well, not really.

As condition for his parole, Gacy relocated to Chicago. He got himself a job, established himself with the Jaycees and relaxed back into society. But he couldn't hold those demons down for long. Within a year or so, he was back before the court for sexually assaulting a teenage boy. But the boy decided not to testify and Gacy was set free.

By 1972, Gacy met another woman, married and began a new life. He started a successful construction business, emerged into the local political scene and had a side job as "Pogo the Clown." He was starting a new version of the American dream.

But Gacy's demons and the lies that hid them became too much to handle and with multiple accusations involving Gacy and teenage boys, he ultimately confessed his sexuality to his wife. Within a year of his coming out, the couple divorced in 1976.

A free man, Gacy went on a binge. Living in his mom's house, Gacy would cruise for young men. Gacy enjoyed forcing himself on young boys. He would routinely overpower the boys or use chloroform to drug them.

Beginning in 1972 and ending in 1978, Gacy went on to kill 33 young males, burying many in a crawl space under his home; others were disposed of in the Des Plaines River. He was found guilty in 1980 and given multiple death penalty and life sentences. He was executed by lethal injection on May 10, 1994.

June 1

"I am the Son of Sam."

Name: David Berkowitz
Nickname: The Son of Sam
Killings: 6
Location: New York City
Years active: 1976-1977
Fun Fact: Berkowitz wrote letters to his neighbor, Craig Glassman. The first began, "Craig Glassman you have been chosen. You have been chosen to die."

June 2

"Like an addiction, you keep craving something that is harder, something which gives you a greater sense of excitement."

Name: Ted Bundy
Killings: 33-36+
Location: United States (scattered)
Years active: 1969 (possibly as early as 1961) - 1978
Fun Fact: Bundy is one of the best known examples of hybristophila. Hybristophilia "is a paraphilia in which sexual arousal, facilitation, and attainment of orgasm are responsive to and contingent upon being with a partner known to have committed an outrage, cheating, lying, known infidelities or crime, such as rape, murder, or armed robbery."

June 3

"They ask, demand, and take. They are drunk from the morning onwards. The question arose of whether these degenerate elements had the right to exist."

Name: Andrei Chikatilo
Nickname: The Butcher of Rostov; The Red Ripper; The Forest Strip Killer; The Rostov Ripper
Killings: 53-56+
Location: Russia
Years active: 1978-1990
Fun Fact: Chikatilo was a late bloomer. He appears to have killed for the first time when he was 42 years old.

June 4

"Happy New Year's, pigs! I've killed four of you motherfuckers. Come on up and I'll kill four more."

Name: Mark James Robert Essex
Killings: 9
Location: New Orleans
Years active: 1972-1973
Fun Fact: The hotel where Essex killed 9 people is still open.

June 5

"I took her into the left bed because the other one had Christmas packages on it. I had intercourse with her…"

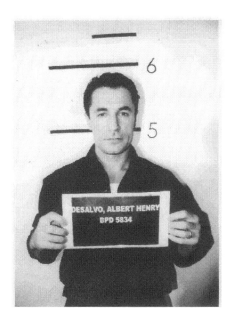

Name: Albert DeSalvo
Nickname: The Boston Strangler
Killings: 13
Location: Boston, MA
Years active: 1962-1964
Fun Fact: There was a popular hardcore/punk band called the Boston Strangler.

June 6

"I choked her to death, then cut her into small pieces so I could take my meat to my rooms, cook and eat it. How sweet and tender her little ass was roasted in the oven. It took me nine days to eat her entire body. I did not fuck her, though I could have, had I wished. She died a virgin."

(Letter to the parents of one victim)

Name: Albert Fish
Nickname/AKA: Thomas Frank Howard
Killings: 10+
Location: New York
Years active: 1924-1932
Fun Fact: Fish loved to write letters. Once he wrote to a woman that was interested in cannibalism. He instructed her tie up her son and husband, whip them daily to tenderize them and then they both would feast.

June 7

"I had a few drinks, I went to bed, and when I woke up the next morning Dick was dead on the floor. I just kept my mouth shut because I didn't want to get involved."

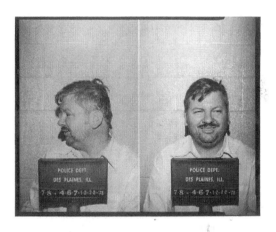

Name: John Wayne Gacy
Nickname: The Killer Clown
Killings: 34
Location: Illinois
Years active: 1972-1978
Fun Fact: Gacy spent a lot of time painting while in prison. You can buy some of his artwork here: http://johnwaynegacyart.com/

June 8

"I began to think about revenging myself on society. I did myself a great deal of damage through reading blood-and-thunder stories, for instance I read the tale of 'Jack the Ripper' several times. When I came to think over what I had read, when I was in prison, I thought what pleasure it would give me to do things of that kind once I got out again."

Name: Peter Kurten
Nickname: The Dusseldorf Vampire
Killings: 9-60
Location: Germany
Years active: 1913-1929
Fun Fact: Before he was 10 years old, Kurten had apparently murdered two schoolmates.

June 9

"Produce your corpses!"

(Mocking the prosecutor in his murder trial)

Name: Henri Desire Landru
Nickname: The Bluebeard of Gambais
Killings: 11
Location: France
Years active: 1915-1919
Fun Fact: Before he began murdering women and taking their assets, Landru was imprisoned for fraud, for doing the same thing without killing them. It must have seemed wiser to leave no victims.

June 10

"I don't remember killing Mama, I just remember hitting her. But they say I did, so I'll go along with that one."

Name: Henry Lee Lucas
Nickname: The Confession Killer
Killings: 3+
Location: United States (scattered)
Years active: 1960-1983
Fun Fact: Lewis injured his eye during a fight when young. His mother ignored the injury for three days, causing Lucas to lose his eye. It was replaced by a glass one.

June 11

"It would be like all the wars that have been fought built one on top of the other, something that no man could conceive of in his imagination. You can't conceive of what it would be like to see every man judge himself and then take it out on every other man all over the face of the earth."

Name: Charles Manson
Killings: 5
Location: California
Years active: 1969
Fun Fact: According to Manson, as a child he was once sold for a pitcher of beer to a childless waitress, from whom his uncle retrieved him some days later.

June 12

"But if old people are without friends or relatives and can't take of themselves, they certainly are better off dead. What's the use of suffering all of the time without a chance of improving? I killed these people and I believe I did the right thing."

Name: Frederick Mors
Nickname: Herr Doktor
Killings: 8
Location: New York
Years active: 1914-1915
Fun Fact: When questioned by police, Mors readily and calmly admitted to killing eight patients that had recently died at a nursing home where he was employed.

June 13

"Herb. I want you to kill me somebody."

(Explaining what the voice he heard telepathically told him.)

Name: Herbert Mullin
Killings: 13
Location: California
Years active: 1972-1973
Fun Fact: Before he started killing, he was hearing voices in his head that told him an earthquake was imminent, and that only through human sacrifice could he save California.

June 14

"It's in there in two plastic bags. It's a long story but I'll tell you everything."

Name: Dennis Nilsen
Nickname: The Kindly Killer
Killings: 15
Location: England
Years active: 1978-1983
Fun Fact: Following his murders, Nilsen would observe a ritual in which he bathed and dressed the victims' bodies, which he would retain for extended periods of time.

June 15

"I reform people."

Name: Carl Panzram
Nickname/AKA: Jefferson Davis
Killings: 22
Location: United States (scattered)
Years active: 1915-1929
Fun Fact: Panzram used several aliases including Jeff Davis,
Jefferson Baldwin, Jack Allen, and John O'Leary.

June 16

"I think I did this not as a sex act, but out of hate for her—not her in particular, but for a woman."

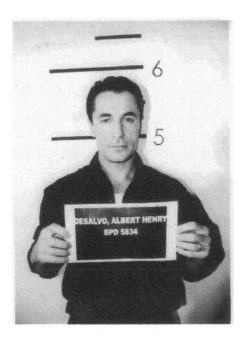

Name: Albert DeSalvo
Nickname: The Boston Strangler
Killings: 13
Location: Boston, MA
Years active: 1962-1964
Fun Fact: DeSalvo supposedly confessed to his cellmate George
Nassar, who also was a murderer, and who at one point was
suspected of being the Boston Strangler.

June 17

"My wife's had another fit, please come at once."

Name: George Joseph Smith
Nickname: Brides in the Bath Murderer
Killings: 3
Location: England
Years active: 1912-1915
Fun Fact: Smith entered into seven bigamous marriages between 1908 and 1914.

June 18

"Only tears of sorrow can wash out the stain of shame; only pangs of suffering can blot out the fires of lust."

(no pic available)

Name: Lucian Staniak
Nickname: The Red Spider
Killings: 6-20
Location: Poland
Years active: 1964-1967
Fun Fact: He was sentenced to death upon his conviction, but it was later overturned when he was ruled insane.

June 19

"Why did it have to happen to me? It is not fair ... it is not right ... why was the world against me?"

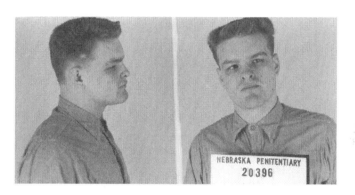

Name: Charles Starkweather
Nickname: Badlands Killer
Killings: 11
Location: Wyoming, Nebraska
Years active: 1957-1958
Fun Fact: Starkweather became angry at his first victim, service station attendant Robert Colvert, for refusing to sell him a stuffed animal on credit.

June 20

"I don't want to explain my actions so that people might like me. I don't even care if people don't like me."

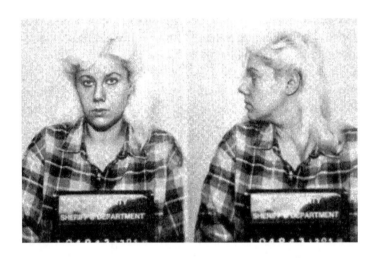

Name: Cathy Wood
Nickname: The Lethal Lovers
Killings: 5
Location: Michigan
Years active: 1987
Fun Fact: Wood is expected to be released from prison in 2021.

June 21

"The most damaging kinds of pornography are those that involve violence and sexual violence. Because the wedding of those two forces, as I know only too well, brings out the hatred that is just, just too terrible to describe."

Name: Ted Bundy
Killings: 33-36+
Location: United States (scattered)
Years active: 1969 (possibly as early as 1961) -1978
Fun Fact: Bundy shoplifted virtually everything that he owned.

June 22

"How proud Charlie would be if I presented him with the baby cut from the womb of the woman."

(Talking about Charles Manson)

Name: Susan Atkins
Nickname: Sadie Mae Glutz
Killings: 5
Location: California
Years active: 1969
Fun Fact: Atkins wrote the famous word "Pig" on the wall in victim Sharon Tate's blood.

June 23

"I am the demon from the bottomless pit here on earth to create havoc and terror. I am War. I am death. I am destruction."

Name: David Berkowitz
Nickname: The Son of Sam
Killings: 6
Location: New York City
Years active: 1976-1977
Fun Fact: Berkowitz claimed to be obeying a demon that manifested itself in his neighbor's dog named "Harvey."

June 24

"This is the Zodiac speaking. I like killing people because it is so much fun."

Name: Zodiac Killer
Nickname: Zodiac Killer
Killings: 5-28
Location: California
Years active: 1960s-1970s
Fun Fact: Although the Zodiac claimed 37 murders in letters to the newspapers, investigators agree on only seven confirmed victims.

June 25

"Dear Boss, I keep on hearing the police have caught me but they won't fix me just yet. I am down on whores and I shan't quit ripping them till I do get buckled. Grand work the last job was. I gave the lady no time to squeal. How can they catch me now?"

(no pic available)

Name: Jack the Ripper
Nickname: The Whitechapel Murderer
Killings: 5+
Location: England
Years active: 1888-1891
Fun Fact: The letter was considered to be genuine, because only a few hours after the infamous double murder on the 30th of September, the police received a postcard referring to the killings. As details of the murders had not been released, all correspondence up to that date was taken seriously.

June 26

"If you try to run, I'll kill the others."

Name: Gary Heidnik
Nickname: Brother Bishop
Killings: 2+
Location: Philadelphia
Years active: 1986-1987
Fun Fact: Heidnik attempted suicide at least 13 times.

June 27

"As for what was said of my life, there have been lies in the past and there will be lies in the future. I don't believe in the hypocritical, moralistic dogma of this so-called civilized society."

Name: Richard Ramirez
Nickname: The Night Stalker
Killings: 14
Location: California
Years active: 1984-1985
Fun Fact: There was another serial killer and rapist known as the "Original Night Stalker" who was never apprehended.

June 28

"The big problem is that people don't believe a revolution is possible, and it is not possible precisely because they do not believe it is possible."

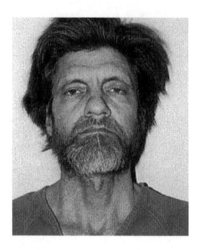

Name: Theodore Kaczynski
Nickname: The Unabomber
Killings: 3 killed, dozens attempted
Location: United States (scattered)
Years active: 1978-1995
Fun Fact: Kaczynski has a tested IQ of 167, suggesting he is among the 1% most intelligent people on earth.

June 29

"I realize I will never function in society again. I don't want to escape, but if I get the chance, I will. I want you to be professional enough to see that I never get the chance."

Name: Ted Bundy
Killings: 33-36+
Location: United States (scattered)
Years active: 1969 (possibly as early as 1961) - 1978
Fun Fact: He sometimes revisited where he brought his victims' bodies for hours at a time, grooming and performing sexual acts with the decomposing corpses.

June 30

"Get out of there before I blow your brains out!"

Name: Frederick W. Cowan
Nickname: Nazi Killer; Neptune Murderer
Killings: 6
Location: New York
Years active: 1977
Fun Fact: Cowan once threatened a neighbor with a gun for dating a black man.

July

July's featured serial killer is David Berkowitz, The Son of Sam.

  If there was ever a time in New York City when its vibrant and exciting nightlife ground to a halt, it was during the summer of 1977. Temperatures soared north of three digits for what seemed like forever. New York City was stifled. With the unending heat, everyone was getting a little tense and crazy. It wasn't just the heat though, the city and its surrounding neighborhoods were suffocated by a psychopath who began indiscriminately gunning down the city's youth; the Son of Sam was born.

  Berkowitz eventually confessed to six killings, originally citing a possessed dog named Harvey as the source of his dementia. Berkowitz claimed that Harvey spoke to him, ordering him to kill. Berkowitz paid attention and followed his neighbor's dog's orders.

Early on David wasn't set up for success. Born David Falco, his mother gave him up for adoption after the married man that she had an affair with threatened to leave her if she kept the child. So, she gave David up to be with her married real estate agent boyfriend.

At a time when others his age were avoiding military service to escape going to Viet Nam, David joined the military in 1971. He was stationed in Korea during his time in the service and was honorably discharged, never seeing a day of combat during the Vietnam War.

After he came back from his stint in the Army, he struggled to find a settled life. Bouncing from menial job to menial job, he ultimately found work as a security guard. It was during this time that he met the dog that would change his life forever.

A labrador retriever named Harvey was owned by his neighbor, Sam Carr. The dog barked a lot... a lot... and that made David a little anxious, to say the least. David penned an angry letter to Harvey's owner, telling him that the barking needed to stop. But the barking didn't stop, the killings began and the Son of Sam was born.

David was eventually caught. He was caught, not because of a smoking gun but because parking in New York is a bitch. He parked his Ford Fairlane too close to a fire hydrant and got a ticket. A resident saw an infuriated man ripping up a parking ticket on the night of one Son of Sam murder. The police, after some prodding, put two and two together and followed up with the owner of the car; a man named David Berkowitz. When the police arrived at his residence, they asked David his name. He said: "I'm Sam."

So the sweltering summer of 1977 came to an end with the capture of The Son of Sam.

David Berkowitz is now a born-again Christian. He actually has a website. Yes... he does. It's www.ariseandshine.org

July 1

"I couldn't find any meaning for my life when I was out there. I'm sure as hell not going to find it in here. This is the grand finale of a life poorly spent and the end result is just overwhelmingly depressing. It's just a sick, pathetic, wretched, miserable life story, that's all it is. How it can help anyone, I've no idea."

Name: Jeffrey Dahmer
Nickname: The Milwaukee Cannibal; The Milwaukee Monster
Killings: 17
Location: Wisconsin
Years active: 1978-1991
Fun Fact: When Dahmer was 16 he devised a plan to lay in wait for a jogger he saw often, hit him in the head with a bat and drag him into the bushes and have sex with his unconscious body. He waited, but the jogger never came.

July 2

"It was like they were already dead to me."

(Speaking of the prostitutes / victims)

Name: Sean Vincent Gillis
Killings: 8
Location: Louisiana
Years active: 1994-2004
Fun Fact: Gillis once claimed he began killing because of "stress."

July 3

"The quest for freedom is death - then by death I shall escape to freedom."

Name: Mark Essex
Killings: 9
Location: New Orleans
Years active: 1972-1973
Fun Fact: A play called "An Evening with Dead Essex," opened in 1973.

July 4

"I am not insane. I am just queer. I don't understand myself."

Name: Albert Fish
Nickname/AKA: Thomas Frank Howard
Killings: 10+
Location: New York
Years active: 1924-1932
Fun Fact: Fish was known to drink urine and eat feces.

July 5

"I'd just as soon shoot you as look at you."

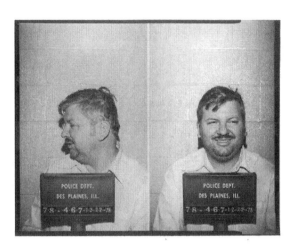

Name: John Wayne Gacy
Nickname: The Killer Clown
Killings: 34
Location: Illinois
Years active: 1972-1978
Fun Fact: Gacy once worked as a mortuary assistant. He claimed to
have learned a lot about dead bodies during this time.

July 6

"Mr. Lusk. Sir, I send you half the Kidney I took from one woman, preserved it for you. The other piece I fried and ate, it was very nice. I may send you the bloody knife that took it out if you only wait a while longer. Signed, Catch me when you can Mister Lusk."

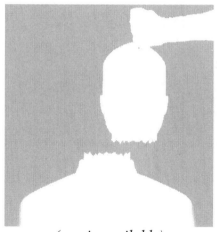

(no pic available)

Name: Jack the Ripper
Nickname: The Whitechapel Murderer
Killings: 5+
Location: England
Years active: 1888-1891
Fun Fact: Despite the many and varied theories about the identity and profession of Jack the Ripper, authorities are not agreed upon any of them and the number of named suspects reaches over one hundred.

July 7

"Even when she was dead, she was still bitching at me. I couldn't get her to shut up."

(Speaking of his mother)

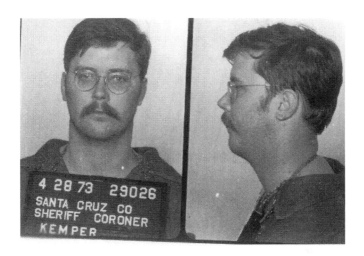

Name: Ed Kemper
Nickname: The Co-Ed Killer
Killings: 10
Location: California
Years active: 1964-1973
Fun Fact: Kemper was a regular at a bar called The Jury Room which was a popular hangout with local law enforcement officers.

July 8

"People were talking about it all around me. All this amount of indignation and horror did me good."

Name: Peter Kurten
Nickname: The Dusseldorf Vampire
Killings: 9-60
Location: Germany
Years active: 1913-1929
Fun Fact: Kurten said to the legal examiners that his primary motive was to "strike back at oppressive society."

July 9

"I got sick about it. I said let's get the hell out of here."

(After showing police the remains of a boy buried in a shallow grave).

Name: Henry Lee Lucas
Nickname: The Confession Killer
Killings: 3+
Location: United States (scattered)
Years active: 1960-1983
Fun Fact: His father lost his legs in a workplace accident and was known as "No Legs" Lucas.

July 10

"Nine black Muslims and three Mexicans signed a writ that said I was Jesus Christ. Is that reality to you as well?"

(At a parole hearing in 1992)

Name: Charles Manson
Killings: 5
Location: California
Years active: 1969
Fun Fact: Manson was once happily married.

July 11

"Hurry it up, you Hoosier bastard. I could kill a dozen men while you're fooling around."

(Speaking to his executioner)

Name: Carl Panzram
Nickname/AKA: Jefferson Davis
Killings: 22
Location: United States (scattered)
Years active: 1915-1929
Fun Fact: Panzram only had one friend in his life, prison guard John Lesser, who Panzram confessed to.

July 12

"She was the one I had to tie really tight. She started to fight. I made it so tight..."

Name: Albert DeSalvo
Nickname: The Boston Strangler
Killings: 13
Location: Boston, MA
Years active: 1962-1964
Fun Fact: DeSalvo was first arrested at 12, for assault and battery, and robbery.

July 13

"They crawl into your very soul, demanding money, food, vodka, and offering themselves for sex. These bums attract minors into their dark net."

(Speaking of his victims)

Name: Andrei Chikatilo
Nickname: The Butcher of Rostov; The Red Ripper; The Forest Strip Killer; The Rostov Ripper
Killings: 53-56+
Location: Russia
Years active: 1978-1990
Fun Fact: Tom Rob Smith's novel "Child 44" was based on Chikatilo.

July 14

"I don't want to have to lie to you."

Name: Ted Bundy
Killings: 33-36+
Location: United States (scattered)
Years active: 1969 (possibly as early as 1961) - 1978
Fun Fact: Bundy loved to ski. To do so he often forged lift tickets and stole ski equipment.

July 15

"The demons wanted girls. Sugar and spice and everything nice."

Name: David Berkowitz
Nickname: The Son of Sam
Killings: 6
Location: New York City
Years active: 1976-1977
Fun Fact: A band named "Son of Sam" featured a member of Danzig.

July 16

"The men and women of this family, my brothers and sisters, have followed me through the killings, to the jails, the courts, to prison, and to Death Row for the love they have for me."

(Speaking of the Manson Family)

Name: Robert Beausoleil
Nickname: Cupid
Killings: 5
Location: California
Years active: 1969
Fun Fact: Beausoleil's good looks made him the Manson Family's main recruiter of young women.

July 17

"Misery leads to crime. I saw so many boys whipped it ruined my mind."

Name: Albert Fish
Nickname/AKA: Thomas Frank Howard
Killings: 10+
Location: New York
Years active: 1924-1932
Fun Fact: At a meeting with reporters after the execution, Fish's lawyer James Dempsey revealed that he was in possession of his client's "final statement." Dempsey refused to show it , stating, "I will never show it to anyone. It was the most filthy string of obscenities that I have ever read."

July 18

"That's their job... to get into a stranger's car."

(Speaking about prostitutes.)

(no pic available)

Name: Joel Rifkin
Killings: 9-17+
Location: New York
Years active: 1974-1991
Fun Fact: Rifkin was involved in a jailhouse dust-up with Long Island Railroad mass murderer Colin Ferguson. Ferguson was using the phone and wanted Rifkin to be quiet. When Rifkin kept talking, Ferguson said, "I wiped out six devils and you only killed women." Rifkin responded, "Yeah, but I had more victims." Ferguson then punched Rifkin in the mouth.

July 19

"I was frustrated in my dreams and desires totally. It was sad, really. I didn't blame society for me not being able to be a policeman."

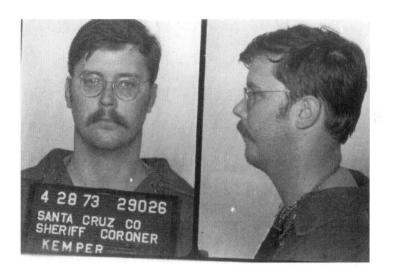

Name: Ed Kemper
Nickname: The Co-Ed Killer
Killings: 10
Location: California
Years active: 1964-1973
Fun Fact: After killing his mother, Kemper cut off her head and used it as a dart board.

July 20

"Do you know where you are? I can tell you! You are alone with me in the middle of the woods. Now you can scream as much as you like and nobody will hear you!"

Name: Peter Kurten
Nickname: The Dusseldorf Vampire
Killings: 9-60
Location: Germnay
Years active: 1913-1929
Fun Fact: In 1931, scientists examined Kurten's brain, looking for irregularities, in an attempt to explain his personality and behavior.

July 21

"I love to kill people. I love watching them die. I would shoot them in the head and they would wiggle and squirm all over the place, and then just stop. Or I would cut them with a knife and watch their faces turn real white. I love all that blood. I told one lady to give me all her money. She said no. So I cut her and pulled her eyes out."

Name: Richard Ramirez
Nickname: The Night Stalker
Killings: 14
Location: California
Years active: 1984-1985
Fun Fact: Ramirez once asked for Sean Penn's autograph through a corrections officer when Penn was in jail.

July 22

"It's kind of rolling country, not flat, and when you get to the edge of it you find these ravines that cut very steeply in to cliff-like drop-offs and there was even a waterfall there. It was about a two days' hike from my cabin. That was the best spot until the summer of 1983. That summer there were too many people around my cabin so I decided I needed some peace. I went back to the plateau and when I got there I found they had put a road right through the middle of it... You just can't imagine how upset I was."

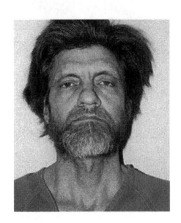

Name: Theodore Kaczynski
Nickname: The Unabomber
Killings: 3 killed, dozens attempted
Location: United States (scattered)
Years active: 1978-1995
Fun Fact: After his arrest, Kaczynski was briefly considered a suspect in the San Francisco Zodiac murders.

July 23

"Tomorrow I will purchase the finest knife money can buy, nothing shall be too good for my whores, I will treat them to the finest, the very finest. They deserve that at least from I."

(no pic available)

Name: Jack the Ripper
Nickname: The Whitechapel Murderer
Killings: 5+
Location: England
Years active: 1888-1891
Fun Fact: Close to 40 movies have been made about Jack the Ripper.

July 24

"My victims never knew what was going to happen to them. I've had shooting, knifings, strangulations, beatings, and I've participated in actual crucifixions of humans. All across the country, there's people just like me, who set out to destroy life."

Name: Henry Lee Lucas
Nickname: The Confession Killer
Killings: 3+
Location: United States (scattered)
Years active: 1960-1983
Fun Fact: Lucas was the only man spared from a Texas death sentence by George W. Bush during Bush's tenure as governor.

July 25

"She passed out fast. I saw purplish-dark blood, it came out of her right ear. I saw it more clearly when I put the pillowcase around her neck, but I strangled her first with my arm, then the pillowcase."

Name: Albert DeSalvo
Nickname: The Boston Strangler
Killings: 13
Location: Boston, MA
Years active: 1962-1964
Fun Fact: DeSalvo is buried in Peabody Massachusetts.

July 26

"I'm sorry for the trouble. Tell the mayor that I'm sorry to be causing the city so much trouble."

Name: Frederick W. Cowan
Nickname: The Nazi Killer
Killings: 6
Location: New York
Years active: 1977
Fun Fact: Cowan idolized Adolf Hitler.

July 27

"Why me? I demand the podium! Get me a lawyer! I didn't confess to anything! Show me the corpses!"

(After receiving the verdict)

Name: Andrei Chikatilo
Nickname: The Butcher of Rostov; The Red Ripper; The Forest Strip Killer; The Rostov Ripper
Killings: 53-56+
Location: Russia
Years active: 1978-1990
Fun Fact: At one point, Chikatilo worked as a teacher. He was largely ineffective. Although knowledgeable in the subjects he taught, he was unable to maintain discipline in his classes and was regularly subjected to mockery by his students.

July 28

"I haven't blocked out the past. I wouldn't trade the person I am, or what I've done - or the people I've known - for anything."

Name: Ted Bundy
Killings: 33-36+
Location: United States (scattered)
Years active: 1969 (possibly as early as 1961) - 1978
Fun Fact: Bundy's fiancée, Liz Kloepfer, confessed that he liked her to pretend to be dead while they were having sex or he couldn't have an orgasm.

July 29

"I am a gladiator against the forces of darkness! I am come into these circumstances so that I might save many lives. I am willing to die to be at peace, to obtain it."

Name: David Berkowitz
Nickname: The Son of Sam
Killings: 6
Location: New York City
Years active: 1976-1977
Fun Fact: Berkowitz didn't bother to show up for his last parole hearing. His next one is in 2016.

July 30

"She was so drunk it only took about a minute and a half to succumb to unconsciousness and then death."

Name: Sean Vincent Gillis
Killings: 8
Location: Louisiana
Years active: 1994-2004
Fun Fact: Gillis kept body parts and photos in his home as souvenirs to stimulate him as he remembered the murders.

July 31

"I have two years left and when I get out I want to become a dentist."

Name: Mark Essex
Killings: 9
Location: New Orleans
Years active: 1972-1973
Fun Fact: Some still believe that there was no way Essex acted alone.

August

August's featured serial killer is Ed Gein.

Ah, Ed Gein. We hardly knew you.

Gein, who has been revered and memorialized in many of the fictional serial killer characters of films and books, is somehow still more disturbed in true-life than his pop-culture representations. Which is a bold statement, considering Ed Gein was the inspiration for Norman Bates (Psycho), Leatherface (Texas Chainsaw Massacre) and Buffalo Bill (Silence of the Lambs).

It's pretty tough to compete with someone would got his rocks off digging up graves and having sex with the corpses. Actually, he disputed the necrophilia, but then again, who wouldn't dispute it?

Gein was not technically a serial killer, because one needs to have reached the magic number of three confirmed kills to qualify. He was only proven to have murdered two people. Even so, he certainly shared many of the same qualities with others who achieved serial killer status.

Early on, Ed's life was centered around his deeply religious mom. Ed's father was an alcoholic and his mom pretty much ran things around the Gein household. She provided for the family by owning and running a local grocery shop. She would teach the kids stories from the bible and preach about the evils of drinking and how women were the work of the devil. Thanks Mrs. Gein…

Ed had an odd infatuation with the dead. He routinely robbed cemeteries of bodies and was rumored to have had sex with them. Although Gein denied having sex with the corpses, saying: "They smelled too bad," what he did to their bodies was almost more disturbing.

Ed didn't like his identity, especially his sexual identity. He wanted to change, but didn't know how to go about it. He lived in a time when sex change operations were not yet available. Instead, he would skin dead women and use the skin to create a new, woman skin for himself. But being a first class seamstress wasn't the only thing Ed did. He was also a furniture maker and a home furnishing creator.

He made leggings, corsets, masks, and dresses from human skin, and a belt from human nipples. He made wastebaskets, a lampshade and chair seats from skins, and he used skulls as the top of bedposts. He also made bowls from human skulls.

Indeed, the inside of Ed's house was so horrifying that upon his arrest, Sheriff Art Schley assaulted him, banging Ed's head several times against a brick wall. By all accounts, Schley was permanently traumatized by what he witnessed at Ed's house. Schley died of heart failure at age 43, just before he was scheduled to testify at Ed's trial.

August 1

"That's the way I like my meat and you'll have to eat it that way too."

(Upon serving raw meat to his children)

Name: Albert Fish
Nickname/AKA: Thomas Frank Howard
Killings: 10+
Location: New York
Years active: 1924-1932
Fun Fact: Fish's sister, brother, mother and uncle all suffered from various forms of mental illness.

August 2

"Everything which I have done makes me tremble."

Name: Andrei Chikatilo
Nickname: The Butcher of Rostov; The Red Ripper; The Forest Strip
Killer; The Rostov Ripper
Killings: 53-56+
Location: Russia
Years active: 1978-1990
Fun Fact: A psychiatric evaluation deemed him sane, with borderline
personality disorder and sadistic tendencies.

August 3

"I like hurting people."

Name: Daniel Camargo Barbosa
Nickname/AKA: Manuel Bulgarin Solis; Beast of the Mangroves
Killings: 72-150
Location: Colombia, Ecuador
Years active: 1974-1986
Fun Fact: Barbosa was murdered in prison by the cousin of one of his victims.

August 4

"The voices stopped. I satisfied the demons' lust."

(Knowing he had killed his victim)

Name: David Berkowitz
Nickname: The Son of Sam
Killings: 6
Location: New York City
Years active: 1976-1977
Fun Fact: Berkowitz was attacked by another inmate in 1979 and received a potentially fatal slash to the left side of his neck that required nearly 60 stitches to close.

August 5

"Everything they've got on me is circumstantial. Do you realize that there's not one person can put me with one of the victims before, during or after the crime?"

(From a man who was discovered with 28 corpses hidden inside his house)

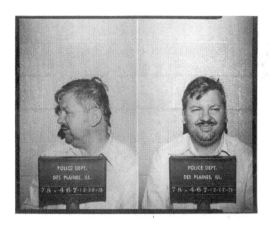

Name: John Wayne Gacy
Nickname: The Killer Clown
Killings: 34
Location: Illinois
Years active: 1972-1978
Fun Fact: Gacy was often a clown at children's parties.

August 6

"I was not codding [joking], dear old Boss, when I gave you the tip. You'll hear about Saucy Jack's work tomorrow. Double event this time. Number one squealed a bit. Couldn't finish straight off. Had not time to get ears for police. Thanks for keeping last letter back till I got to work again."

(no pic available)

Name: Jack the Ripper
Nickname: The Whitechapel Murderer
Killings: 5+
Location: England
Years active: 1888-1891
Fun Fact: Alice in Wonderland author Lewis Carroll was a suspect in the Jack the Ripper murders.

August 7

"If I were seeing this patient without having any history available or without getting the history from him, I would think that we're dealing with a very well adjusted young man who had initiative, intelligence and who was free of any psychiatric illness."

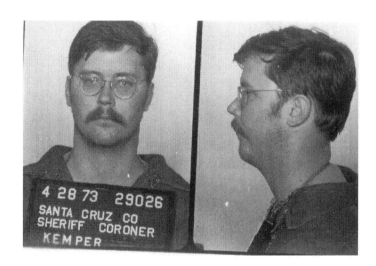

Name: Ed Kemper
Nickname: The Co-Ed Killer
Killings: 10
Location: California
Years active: 1964-1973
Fun Fact: Despite his gigantic physical size, Kemper supposedly has a small penis.

August 8

"The sight of the flames delighted me, but above all it was the excitement of the attempts to extinguish the fire and the agitation of those who saw their property being destroyed."

Name: Peter Kurten
Nickname: The Dusseldorf Vampire
Killings: 9-60
Location: Germany
Years active: 1913-1929
Fun Fact: At one point Kurten was employed as a dogcatcher.

August 9

"I wonder if there is any lady present who would care to take my seat?"

(Before leaving the courtroom for the last time)

Name: Henri Desire Landru
Nickname: The Bluebeard of Gambais
Killings: 11
Location: France
Years active: 1915-1919
Fun Fact: Landru was executed by guillotine.

August 10

"You wasn't a cannibal. It's the force of the devil, something forced on us that we can't change. There's no reason denying what we become. We know what we are. Ottis, you know everything you say is going on tape here?"

Name: Henry Lee Lucas
Nickname: The Confession Killer
Killings: 3+
Location: United States (scattered)
Years active: 1960-1983
Fun Fact: Lucas is buried in Peckerwood Hill Cemetery.

August 11

"Don't worry, I'm not going to hurt you black people, I want the whites."

Name: Mark James Robert Essex
Killings: 9
Location: New Orleans
Years active: 1972-1973
Fun Fact: Essex went AWOL from the Navy.

August 12

"Poor woman, she died of overexertion."

Name: Raymond Martinez
Nickname: Lonely Hearts Bandit
Killings: 5-17
Location: New York
Years active: 1947-1949
Fun Fact: His partner in murder was a woman named Martha Beck.
She had this to say as her official last words: "My story is a love
story. But only those tortured by love can know what I mean.
Imprisonment in the Death House has only strengthened my feeling
for Raymond."

August 13

"I freed their soul from suffering. Nuisances, all of them!"

Name: Frederick Mors
Nickname: Herr Doktor
Killings: 8
Location: New York
Years active: 1914-1915
Fun Fact: Mors initially used arsenic, opium, and morphine to poison his victims.

August 14

"I wish you all had one neck, and I had my hands on it."

(In a letter to anti-death penalty activists who tried to petition to get his execution stayed)

Name: Carl Panzram
Nickname/AKA: Jefferson Davis
Killings: 22
Location: United States (scattered)
Years active: 1915-1929
Fun Fact: At various points in his life, Panzram served time in prisons in Minnesota (reform school as a child), California, Texas, Oregon, Idaho, Montana, Connecticut, New York, Washington D.C., and the federal prison at Leavenworth, Kansas.

August 15

"I need not look beyond this room to see all the liars, haters, the killers, the crooks, the paranoid cowards - truly trematodes of the earth, each one in his own legal profession."

Name: Richard Ramirez
Nickname: The Night Stalker
Killings: 14
Location: California
Years active: 1984-1985
Fun Fact: Ramirez once had a job at a Holiday Inn, where he used his passkey to rob sleeping hotel guests.

August 16

"One night she blew it, screamed at me, said I'd tried to scare her to get her to have a heart attack, kill her."

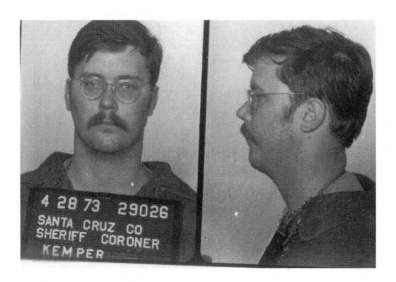

Name: Ed Kemper
Nickname: The Co-Ed Killer
Killings: 10
Location: California
Years active: 1964-1973
Fun Fact: Kemper killed his grandparents when he was 15 because he wanted to know what it felt like.

August 17

"The head will come off next time, also the whore's hands. Shall I leave them in various places around Whitechapel? The Bitch. She will suffer but not as yet. Tomorrow I travel to London. I have decided I cannot wait any longer. I look forward to tomorrow night's work. It will do me good, a great deal of good."

(no pic available)

Name: Jack the Ripper
Nickname: The Whitechapel Murderer
Killings: 5+
Location: England
Years active: 1888-1891
Fun Fact: Jack the Ripper only killed prostitutes.

August 18

"Rich people could do all kinds of sex things and get away with it. They just bought their way out."

Name: Albert DeSalvo
Nickname: The Boston Strangler
Killings: 13
Location: Boston, MA
Years active: 1962-1964
Fun Fact: As a boy, DeSalvo was taught to shoplift by his father.

August 19

"I will be responsibil [sic] for these crimes and no one else. It all started when I wondered what it would be like to kill someone. And I found out. What a nightmare it has been."

Name: Keith Hunter Jesperson
Nickname: The Happy Face Killer
Killings: 8+
Location: United States (scattered)
Years active: 1990-1995
Fun Fact: Jesperson signed numerous confessions to his murders with a smiley face.

August 20

"But I'm the most cold-hearted son of a bitch you'll ever meet."

Name: Ted Bundy
Killings: 33-36+
Location: United States (scattered)
Years active: 1969 (possibly as early as 1961) - 1978
Fun Fact: Bundy may have murdered more than 100 people. Long periods of his life remain unaccounted for, and he is a suspect in more than a dozen murders for which he was never put on trial. Minutes before his execution, investigators were still questioning him about his role in unsolved homicides.

August 21

"The demons were protecting me. I had nothing to fear from the police."

Name: David Berkowitz
Nickname: The Son of Sam
Killings: 6
Location: New York City
Years active: 1976-1977
Fun Fact: Elliot Smith wrote a song called "Son of Sam."

August 22

"I went out... to fetch some eggs for our breakfast... when I returned... I found my sweetheart... dead."

Name: George Joseph Smith
Nickname: Brides in the Bath Murderer
Killings: 3
Location: England
Years active: 1912-1915
Fun Fact: The Smith case was mentioned in Agatha Christie's novels *A Caribbean Mystery* and *The Murder on the Links.*

August 23

"They had me numbered for the bottom."

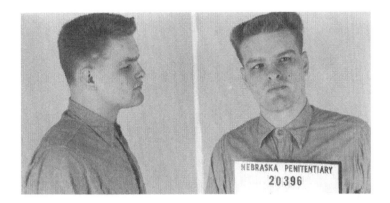

Name: Charles Starkweather
Nickname: Badlands Killer
Killings: 11
Location: Wyoming, Nebraska
Years active: 1957-1958
Fun Fact: Starkweather first claimed that his girlfriend Caril Ann
Fugate was captured by him and had nothing to do with the murders.
However, he changed his story several times, finally testifying at
Fugate's trial that she was a willing participant.

August 24

"I developed and played up on a hatred for prostitutes."

Name: Peter Sutcliffe
Nickname: The Yorkshire Ripper
Killings: 13
Location: England
Years active: 1975-1980
Fun Fact: Sutcliffe was diagnosed as suffering from paranoid schizophrenia.

August 25

"I had learned that a boy's penis could be used for something besides to urinate with and that rectum could be used for other purposes than crepitating."

Name: Carl Panzram
Nickname/AKA: Jefferson Davis
Killings: 22
Location: United States (scattered)
Years active: 1915-1929
Fun Fact: Panzram was a fan of getting inked long before it went mainstream. His body was covered in tattoos, including a giant eagle on his chest and the words LIBERTY and JUSTICE under his pectoral muscles.

August 26

"I might have implied on several different occasions to several different people that I may have been Jesus Christ, but I haven't yet decided what I am or who I am."

Name: Charles Manson
Killings: 5
Location: California
Years active: 1969
Fun Fact: Manson borrowed philosophically from the Process Church, whose members thought Satan would become reconciled with Christ, and they would come together at the end of the world to judge humanity.

August 27

"I followed the woman from the convenience store, to a driveway she pulled into. And I hung around several hours, till it come wee hours of the morning. Then I went into this house. I go to the first bedroom I see. I don't know whose room it is and, and, and, and I start stabbing."

Name: Tommy Lynn Sells
Nickname: The Cross Country Killer
Killings: 22+
Location: United States (scattered)
Years active: 1980-1999
Fun Fact: Sells was diagnosed with a personality disorder consisting of antisocial, borderline, and schizoid features, substance use disorder, bipolar disorder, major depressive disorder, and psychosis.

August 28

"And I've got 100 more out there somewhere!"

(Admitting in a North Texas courtroom he had killed an 80-year-old woman)

Name: Henry Lee Lucas
Nickname: The Confesion Killer
Killings: 3+
Location: United States (scattered)
Years active: 1960-1983
Fun Fact: Lucas' mother was a prostitute, who would force him to watch her have sex with clients.

August 29

"It is 25. I had 25 victims, but they can find only nine bodies. You underrate me. I am Germany's greatest killer. I put others, both here and abroad, to shame."

Name: Rudolf Pleil
Nickname: The Deathmaker
Killings: 10-25
Location: Germany
Years active: 1946-1947
Fun Fact: Pleil had an accomplice who helped him trap victims. They had a falling out because Pleil felt that his accomplice was "barbaric" for wanting to decapitate one of them.

August 30

"Because of my own character — reserved, timid, shy, especially in childhood, I am not able to adapt to this society and live my own life."

Name: Andrei Chikatilo
Nickname: The Butcher of Rostov; The Red Ripper; The Forest Strip Killer; The Rostov Ripper
Killings: 53-56+
Location: Russia
Years active: 1978-1990
Fun Fact: There was a devastating famine in Ukraine when Chikatilo was growing up. He claimed not to have eaten bread until the age of twelve, adding that he and his family often had to eat grass and leaves.

August 31

"One whore in heaven, two whores side by side, three whores all have died, so help me God my next will be far the worst, my head aches."

(no pic available)

Name: Jack the Ripper
Nickname: The Whitechapel Murderer
Killings: 5+
Location: England
Years active: 1888-1891
Fun Fact: Two murders occurred on the same night, which experts dubbed the "Double Event."

September

September's featured serial killer is Aileen Wuornos.

    If this were the late 1980s and you were a guy driving down a dusty, out-of-the-way back road somewhere in the middle of Florida and came across a hitchhiker that was kind of hard on the eyes and a lot off of her rocker, you might not be alive today. Nowadays you can find lookalikes in Walmart, but back then, Aileen Wuornos was one of a kind.

    She hitchhiked the back roads in an effort to offer her services to weary travelers. By services, I mean blowjobs by the side of the road. Often, she would rob her clients and sometimes take their car… and those were just the lucky ones. For seven unlucky travelers it didn't work out even that well. They lost their money all right. But they also found themselves at the business end of a cheap handgun and later face down in a ditch.

Aileen was one of the first well-known female serial killers. Although female serial killers are in the minority (roughly 17% of all serial killers are female), Aileen gained significant notoriety because of the media hailstorm during 1989 and 1990. She was one the first serial killers that the 24-hour cable news cycle latched onto and made into a celebrity of murder. She might not have been TV ready, but she sure was compelling TV.

One thing of note about Aileen; she hated men. She really, really, hated men. Like many serial killers, she survived a childhood of horrific abuse at the hands of men. The seven men that she killed were shot with an average of more than 5 bullets per victim.

The movie Monster, starring Charlize Theron, was based on Wuornos's life. Theron won best actress for her portrayal of the whacked-out serial killer.

Aileen, who knew the penal system pretty well, was finally arrested at The Last Resort, a biker bar in Volusia County, Florida.

She was executed in 2002.

September 1

"I don't remember killing anyone. I could have done it without knowing it. I am not sure if I did it."

Name: Kenneth Erskine
Nickname: The Stockwell Strangler
Killings: 11
Location: England
Years active: 1986
Fun Fact: When on trial Erskine was scolded by the court for falling asleep during the proceedings and, at one point, snoring.

September 2

"I have a sex problem. I just crave women all the time."

Name: Henry Lee Lucas
Nickname: The Confession Killer
Killings: 3+
Location: United States (scattered)
Years active: 1960-1983
Fun Fact: Lucas claimed his mother smashed a two-by-four across the back of his head when he was seven.

September 3

"There is no doubt in my mind, that demon has been living in me since birth."

Name: David Berkowitz
Nickname: Son of Sam
Killings: 6
Location: New York City
Years active: 1976-1977
Fun Fact: A book about downstairs neighbor Craig Glassman, who Berkowitz taunted in letters and who died in a car accident in 1991, is titled Off the Wall. Due to a very limited print run, it has become a collector's item, currently selling for around $300 on Amazon.

September 4

"They take everything from you, everything. Your dignity, your pride. What can you do but hate them?"

Name: Mark Essex
Killings: 9
Location: New Orleans
Years active: 1972-1973
Fun Fact: In the Navy, Essex was a training to be a dentist.

September 5

"She isn't missing. She's at the farm right now."

Name: Ed Gein
Nickname: The Mad Butcher
Killings: 2+
Location: Wisconsin
Years active: 1954-1957
Fun Fact: Soon after his mother's death, Gein began to create a "woman suit" so "he could become his mother — literally crawl into her skin."

September 6

"First I committed sodomy on him and then I killed him."

Name: Carl Panzram
Nickname/AKA: Jefferson Davis
Killings: 22
Location: United States (scattered)
Years active: 1915-1929
Fun Fact: In his autobiography Panzram stated, "Whenever I met one that wasn't too rusty looking I would make him raise his hands and drop his pants. I wasn't very particular either. I rode them old and young, tall and short, white and black. It made no difference to me at all except that they were human beings."

September 7

"You maggots make me sick, hypocrites one and all."

Name: Richard Ramirez
Nickname: The Night Stalker
Killings: 14
Location: California
Years active: 1984-1985
Fun Fact: Ramirez was caught by an angry mob. Authorities released his prior mug shots to the public, and within a couple days a crowd in East L.A. had captured Ramirez while he was trying to steal a car. Cops had to intervene to prevent the mob from beating Ramirez to death.

September 8

"I've prepared a nice, hot bath for you, dearest."

Name: George Joseph Smith
Nickname: Brides in the Bath Murderer
Killings: 3
Location: England
Years active: 1912-1915
Fun Fact: Smith was first sent to a reformatory at the age of 9.

September 9

"Shooting people was, I guess, a kind of thrill. It brought out something."

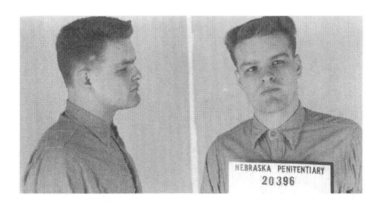

Name: Charles Starkweather
Nickname: Badlands Killer
Killings: 11
Location: Wyoming, Nebraska
Years active: 1957-1958
Fun Fact: The movie "Badlands" is based on Starkweather's crimes.

September 10

"I enjoyed taking care of those old people."

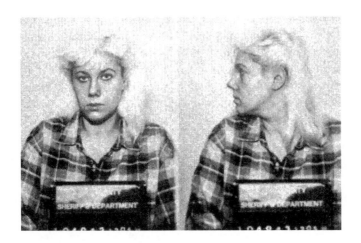

Name: Cathy Wood
Nickname: The Lethal Lovers
Killings: 5
Location: Michigan
Years active: 1987
Fun Fact: During her trial, Wood got a reduced sentence claiming that it was her girlfriend who planned and carried out the killings while Wood served as a lookout or distracted supervisors.

September 11

"You're an inhuman bunch of fucking bastards and bitches and you're gonna get your asses nuked in the end.... and pretty soon it's comin'."

Name: Aileen Wuornos
Killings: 7
Location: Florida
Years active: 1989-1990
Fun Fact: Wuornos's father was a schizophrenic who was jailed for sex crimes against children. He hanged himself in his cell when Wuornos was 13 years old. The two never met.

September 12

"I gave up love and happiness a long time ago."

Name: Richard Ramirez
Nickname: The Night Stalker
Killings: 14
Location: California
Years active: 1984-1985
Fun Fact: His victims ranged from 9 years old to 83.

September 13

"I don't believe in man, God nor Devil. I hate the whole damned human race, including myself. I preyed upon the weak, the harmless and the unsuspecting. This lesson I was taught by others: Might makes right."

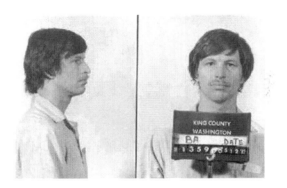

Name: Gary Ridgway
Nickname: The Green River Killer; Green River Gary; The River Man
Killings: 49-90+
Location: Washington
Years active: 1982-2001
Fun Fact: When questioned about Ridgway after his arrest, friends and family described him as friendly but strange.

September 14

"There's no slack in my act."

Name: Charles Manson
Killings: 5
Location: California
Years active: 1969
Fun Fact: Rumor has it that Manson wanted to kill Frank Sinatra
and Steve McQueen.

September 15

"They ain't got, I don't think, a human being alive that can say he had the childhood I had."

Name: Henry Lee Lucas
Nickname: The Confession Killer
Killings: 3+
Location: United States (scattered)
Years active: 1960-1983
Fun Fact: The 1986 movie: "Henry, Portrait of a Serial Killer" is based on Lucas.

September 16

"I did it out of love. I was like a runaway plane, no control, such a rage."

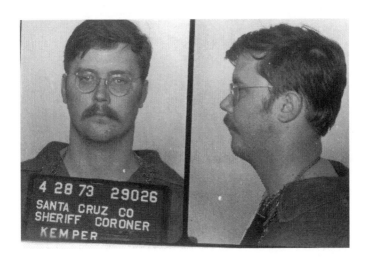

Name: Ed Kemper
Nickname: The Co-Ed Killer
Killings: 10
Location: California
Years active: 1964-1973
Fun Fact: Kemper requested the death penalty. Being executed was apparently a childhood fantasy of his. His request was denied, and as of 2015, he is alive and in prison.

September 17

"I emptied the gun and I was still pulling the trigger and it was clicking, but I didn't know it… I went straight home and went to bed."

Name: David Berkowitz
Nickname: The Son of Sam
Killings: 6
Location: New York City
Years active: 1976-1977
Fun Fact: His first victim was an unknown female who was stabbed from behind on Christmas Eve, 1975. She survived.

September 18

"There has got to be some kind of explanation as to why this has all happened."

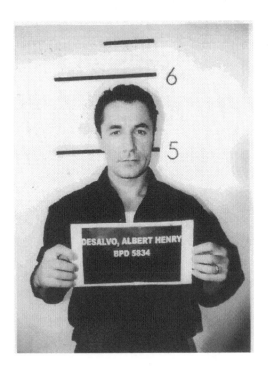

Name: Albert De Salvo
Nickname: The Boston Strangler
Killings: 13
Location: Boston, MA
Years active: 1962-1964
Fun Fact: DeSalvo was discharged from the military for molesting a child.

September 19

"I did not kill either people I hated or people I loved. I killed whoever crossed my path at the moment my urge for murder took hold of me."

Name: Peter Kurten
Nickname: The Dusseldorf Vampire
Killings: 9-60
Location: Germany
Years active: 1913-1929
Fun Fact: When the Nazis rose to power, one of their selling points was that they would crack down on degenerates like Kurten.

September 20

"You must avenge me!"

(Screamed to his horrified wife as he was led from court after the guilty verdict)

Name: Dr. Marcel Andre Petiot
Nickname: Doctor Satan
Killings: 27-63
Location: France
Years active: 1926-1944
Fun Fact: Petiot was guillotined in Paris. His execution was delayed a few days because of a malfunction with the guillotine.

September 21

"What alcohol did in conjunction with exposure to pornography… is alcohol reduced my inhibitions at the same time the fantasy life that was fueled by pornography eroded them further."

Name: Ted Bundy
Killings: 33-36+
Location: United States (scattered)
Years active: 1969 (possibly as early as 1961) - 1978
Fun Fact: Bundy is probably responsible for the murder of an 8 year old girl who disappeared when he was a 15 year old paperboy. She was known to follow Bundy around "like a puppy."

September 22

"I was very angry with that girl. I dreamed of catching her and tearing her to pieces as a revenge for my disaster."

Name: Andrei Chikatilo
Nickname: The Butcher of Rostov; The Red Ripper; The Forest Strip
Killer; The Rostov Ripper
Killings: 53-56+
Location: Russia
Years active: 1978-1990
Fun Fact: Chikalito was arrested under suspicion of being the
Rostov serial killer in September 1984. He was released in
December 1984 for lack of evidence, and had resumed his activities
by July 1985. His last known murder was in February 1990.

September 23

"It's even bigger than you and I, even bigger than God."

Name: Mark Essex
Killings: 9
Location: New Orleans
Years active: 1972-1973
Fun Fact: Although supposedly out to kill only white people, the first person Essex killed was a black policeman.

September 24

"The eyes will come out of the next. I will stuff them in the whore's mouth. That will certainly give me pleasure, it does so as I write. Tonight I will see mine, she will be pleased as I will be gentle with her as indeed I always am."

(no pic available)

Name: Jack the Ripper
Nickname: The Whitechapel Murderer
Killings: 5+
Location: England
Years active: 1888-1891
Fun Fact: One can still visit the graves of Jack the Ripper's victims.

September 25

"One second she's animated and next second she's not. Just a noise and absolute, absolute stillness."

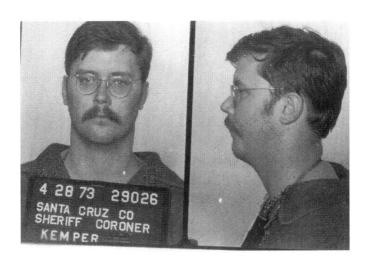

Name: Ed Kemper
Nickname: The Co-Ed Killer
Killings: 10
Location: California
Years active: 1964-1973
Fun Fact: Kemper almost always cut off the heads of his victims.

September 26

"I told them I cut this one girl up in pieces and made hamburger out of her. I didn't do any such thing."

Name: Henry Lee Lucas
Nickname: The Confession Killer
Killings: 3+
Location: United States (scattered)
Years active: 1960-1983
Fun Fact: Lucas met fellow murderer and partner-in-crime Ottis Toole at a soup kitchen.

September 27

"You have to slow down with my mind and to - to see where your mind is."

Name: Charles Manson
Killings: 5
Location: California
Years active: 1969
Fun Fact: Although Manson never killed anyone himself, he did shoot a man named Bernard Crowe, who survived.

September 28

"First, I would pour a drop or two of chloroform on a piece of absorbent cotton and hold it to the nostrils of the old person I wanted to assist out of the world. Soon my man would swoon. Then I would close the orifices of the body with cotton, stuffing it in the ears, nostrils, etc. Next I would pour a little chloroform down the throat and prevent the fumes from escaping the same way. It wasn't long before the heart stopped beating."

Name: Frederick Mors
Nickname: Herr Doktor
Killings: 8
Location: New York
Years active: 1914-1915
Fun Fact: Mors was not suspected of any crimes until he confessed.

September 29

"I tried a little sodomy on him first... I left him laying there with his brains coming out of his ears."

Name: Carl Panzram
Nickname/AKA: Jefferson Davis
Killings: 22
Location: United States (scattered)
Years active: 1915-1929
Fun Fact: By the age of 14, Panzram was a hobo traveling by freight train. Early in his travels, he claimed to have been gang-raped by a group of adult male hobos.

September 30

"I love my work. Now the void has been filled."

Name: David Berkowitz
Nickname: The Son of Sam
Killings: 6
Location: New York City
Years active: 1976-1977
Fun Fact: It was suspected that his first murder could have been a
mafia hit, since it was done in an area where a lot of Italians lived.

October

October's featured serial killer is Dennis Rader.

Dennis Rader is known at the BTK killer. BTK stands for "bind, torture, kill," which was his modus operandi. He was one of the more dark, ominous and most feared serial killers of recent memory. Why? Well, because he seemed like a real normal dude. He was the kind of guy that you would stand behind on a checkout line in a grocery store (or at a pornography store, which he was known to frequent).

Dennis Rader had a normal job, working for a nationwide Home Security company, installing and maintaining home security panels. Let me repeat that – a serial killer installed home security systems for a living.

He lived and socialized in the same community that he terrorized. He hid in plain sight. This guy could blend into the background because of his bland appearance and ultra-normal persona. You would never know who Dennis really was until you met him on one of his bad nights; on those nights, you would end up Bound, Tortured and Killed.

During the BTK's reign of terror, which spanned from 1974 to 1991, the area in and around Wichita, Kansas never settled down. Then he stopped killing. Eventually the police files dusted over and BTK faded away into people's memories. But BTK's ego got the better of him. He loved the spotlight. He loved the notoriety. He needed the attention. So like all sociopaths, he sought it out.

He sent letters and packages to the media. When nothing really came from the media, BTK sent what amounted to gifts to the police. In one package, he sent a 1.44 megabyte computer disk to the police (the historians among you will remember when computers had floppy disks). Police were able to resurrect a previously deleted file that led them directly back to Rader.

In the end, the BTK Killer was responsible for ten murders. He is now serving out his life in prison. But one may wonder, with his knot-making skills, whether he could make one good solid rope to escape.

October 1

"I am beyond your experience. I am beyond good and evil, legions of the night—night breed. Repeat not the errors of the Night Stalker and show no mercy."

Name: Richard Ramirez
Nickname: The Night Stalker
Killings: 14
Location: California
Years active: 1984-1985
Fun Fact: When captured by an angry mob, Ramirez was shouting "Dejame en paz! Dejame en paz!" — Spanish for "Leave me in peace." He thanked arriving officers for rescuing him.

October 2

"The house I have rented with my wife has no bath. She simply will not put up with the lack of such a necessity an hour longer."

Name: George Joseph Smith
Nickname: Brides in the Bath Murderer
Killings: 3
Location: England
Years active: 1912-1915
Fun Fact: The Brides in the Bath was made into a popular television show on Yorkshire Television.

October 3

"The world is lifeless anyhow, like the people I killed."

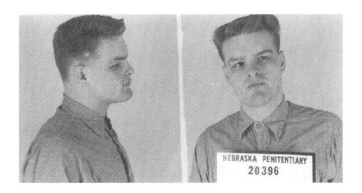

Name: Charles Starkweather
Nickname: Badlands Killer
Killings: 11
Location: Wyoming, Nebraska
Years active: 1957-1958
Fun Fact: In response to a 2012 Casper Star-Tribune article on Starkweather and his girlfriend and accomplice Caril Ann Fugate, one online commenter posted Fugate's full name, address, phone number and recent marriage information.

October 4

"I know... Remember how I liked to pour some blood out on them?"

Name: Ottis Toole
Killings: 6+
Location: Florida
Years active: 1975-1983
Fun Fact: Toole once married a woman 25 years older than him. She left him after three days when she discovered he was gay.

October 5

"When they were asleep I would get my .45 Colt Army Automatic and blow their brains out."

Name: Carl Panzram
Nickname/AKA: Jefferson Davis
Killings: 22
Location: United States (scattered)
Years active: 1915-1929
Fun Fact: In 1910, Panzram went to Mexico to join the rebel leader Pascual Orozco. He witnessed the wholesale slaughter of prisoners by Orozco during the Mexican revolution.

October 6

"Here's a man who is accused of murdering hundreds of thousands in Vietnam who is accusing me of being guilty of eight murders."

(Referring to President Richard Nixon)

Name: Charles Manson
Killings: 5
Location: California
Years active: 1969
Fun Fact: Manson was born to an unmarried 16-year-old girl named Kathleen Maddox. His name at birth was "no name Maddox." It remains unclear who his biological father was.

October 7

**"I was death on women. I don't feel they need to exist.
I hated them, and I wanted to destroy every one I could
find. I was doing a good job of it. I've killed 360
people, in 36 states, in three different countries."**

Name: Henry Lee Lucas
Nickname: The Confession Killer
Killings: 3+
Location: United States (scattered)
Years active: 1960-1983
Fun Fact: In 1985, just a couple years into his incarceration, he
attempted to tell his story in a book, written for him by a sympathetic
author. The book was titled "The Hand of Death: The Henry Lee
Lucas Story."

October 8

"There was blood from the right nostril... like a faucet. One eye was open, one shut. I wrapped her head with a towel and put her down. I dragged her into the bedroom."

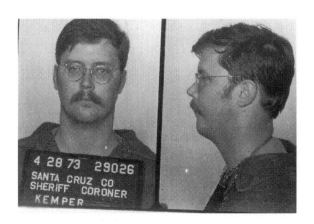

Name: Ed Kemper
Nickname: The Co-Ed Killer
Killings: 10
Location: California
Years active: 1964-1973
Fun Fact: Kemper shot his grandmother with the rifle that his grandfather bought for him.

October 9

"Hey, I got a lot of important work to do. I can't be going down to the police station. I know this kid is missing but that's not important to me."

Name: John Wayne Gacy
Nickname: The Killer Clown
Killings: 34
Location: Illinois
Years active: 1972-1978
Fun Fact: Dr. Helen Morrison possesses a piece of Gacy's brain.

October 10

"I'm not educated and these girls was all college graduates, understand me? I made fools of them... I made them do what I wanted and accept me and listen to me."

Name: Albert DeSalvo
Nickname: The Boston Strangler
Killings: 13
Location: Boston, MA
Years active: 1962-1964
Fun Fact: DeSalvo was incarcerated for the "Green Man" rapes, so called because he always wore green work pants and a green shirt.

October 11

"If something was wrong in my life and my work, then I found myself again at the train station or in the forest, and so all that would start. That frustration pressured me all the time and it was boiling inside of me every day, every hour."

Name: Andrei Chikatilo
Nickname: The Butcher of Rostov; The Red Ripper; The Forest Strip Killer; The Rostov Ripper
Killings: 53-56+
Location: Russia
Years active: 1978-1990
Fun Fact: Chikatilo was executed in 1994. No electric chair or lethal injection for him. This was Russia, after all. He was taken to a soundproof room and killed with a single gunshot to the back of the head.

October 12

"I didn't feel socially adept enough. I didn't feel I knew how to function with those people. I felt terribly uncomfortable."

Name: Ted Bundy
Killings: 33-36+
Location: United States (scattered)
Years active: 1969 (possibly as early as 1961) - 1978
Fun Fact: Some theorize that Bundy is responsible for 150 deaths.

October 13

"I would talk to her... and get her mind off of the sex, anything she was nervous about. And think, you know, she thinks, 'Oh, this guy cares'... which I didn't. I just want to, uh, get her in the vehicle and eventually kill her."

Name: Gary Ridgway
Nickname: The Green River Killer
Killings: 49-90+
Location: Washington
Years active: 1982-2001
Fun Fact: Ridgway became a suspect in the Green River killings in 1983. In 1984, he took and passed a lie detector test.

October 14

"You hear that little pop and pull their heads off and hold their heads up by the hair. Whipping their heads off, their body sitting there. That'd get me off."

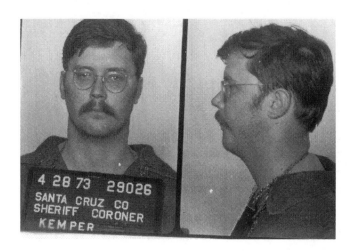

Name: Ed Kemper
Nickname: The Co-Ed Killer
Killings: 10
Location: California
Years active: 1964-1973
Fun Fact: Kemper committed his crimes in the same area and around the same time as two other serial killers, John Linley Frazier and Herbert Mullins. At the time, the Santa Cruz area became known as the "Murder Capital of the World."

October 15

"It was their fate to die by my hands, like a car accident or illness."

Name: Keith Hunter Jesperson
Nickname: The Happy Face Killer
Killings: 8+
Location: United States (scattered)
Years active: 1990-1995
Fun Fact: In January 1995, Jesperson agreed to give a young woman, Angela Surbrize, a lift from Spokane, Washington, to Indiana. Approximately a week into the trip, Surbrize became impatient and began to nag Jesperson to hurry up, as she wanted to see her boyfriend. In response, Jesperson raped and strangled her.

October 16

"I saw monsters often and I heard them, which often caused me to go screaming hysterically into my parents' room... Now I know that they were real."

Name: David Berkowitz
Nickname: The Son of Sam
Killings: 6
Location: New York City
Years active: 1976-1977
Fun Fact: Berkowitz was adopted.

October 17

"There is no place in this white man's navy for a self-respecting black man."

Name: Mark Essex
Killings: 9
Location: New Orleans
Years active: 1972-1973
Fun Fact: Essex was a member of the Black Panthers.

October 18

"Killing became the same thing as having sex."

Name: Henry Lee Lucas
Nickname: The Confession Killer
Killings: 3+
Location: United States (scattered)
Years active: 1960-1983
Fun Fact: Lucas claimed at one point he was part of a cult called "The Hand of Death."

October 19

"I'm a gangster and I'm bad and I'm all the things that I want to be. I'm pretty free within myself. I cut people and I shoot them and I do whatever I have to do to survive in the world I live in. But that has nothing to do with me breaking the law."

Name: Charles Manson
Killings: 5
Location: California
Years active: 1969
Fun Fact: Manson was supposed to be married recently. But now, sadly, the wedding appears to be off as the woman just wanted to marry him so she could display his body after he dies.

October 20

"It was a very simple matter—the killing of these useless old people. The only difficulty I had was in devising a way to prevent the fumes of chloroform from escaping into the air of the room and becoming noticeable to anyone who entered."

Name: Frederick Mors
Nickname: Herr Doktor
Killings: 8
Location: New York
Years active: 1914-1915
Fun Fact: Mors's real name was Carl Menarik.

October 21

"By killing them, I'm the man who goes around doing good."

Name: Carl Panzram
Nickname/AKA: Jefferson Davis
Killings: 22
Location: United States (scattered)
Years active: 1915-1929
Fun Fact: After Panzram's death, friend and jail guard Henry Lesser attempted to publish Panzram's autobiography and dedicated his life to prison reform.

October 22

"Serial killers do, on a small scale, what governments do on a large one. They are products of our times."

Name: Richard Ramirez
Nickname: The Night Stalker
Killings: 14
Location: California
Years active: 1984-1985
Fun Fact: Ramirez broke into the apartment of Bill Carns, 29, and his fiancée, Inez Erickson, 27. Ramirez shot Carns in the head and raped Erickson. He demanded she swear her love for Satan and afterward forced her to perform oral sex on him. He then tied her and left. Erickson struggled to get to the window and saw the car Ramirez was driving. She was able to give police a description of both Ramirez and his orange Toyota station wagon. This led to his capture a few days later. Carns survived.

October 23

"I may be a bit peculiar but I am certainly no murderer!"

Name: George Joseph Smith
Nickname: Brides in the Bath Murderer
Killings: 3
Location: England
Years active: 1912-1915
Fun Fact: Smith entered into seven bigamous marriages between 1908 and 1914.

October 24

"They said they were tired of me hanging around. I told Mrs. Bartlett off and she got so mad that she slapped me. When I hit her back, her husband started to come at me, so I had to let both of them have it with my rifle."

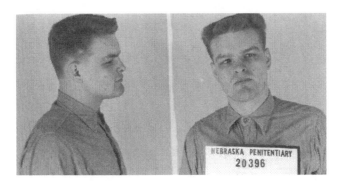

Name: Charles Starkweather
Nickname: Badlands Killer
Killings: 11
Location: Wyoming, Nebraska
Years active: 1957-1958
Fun Fact: After Starkweather killed his girlfriend Caril Fugate's family, Fugate put up a note on the front door of the house that said, "Stay away, everybody is sick with the flu."

October 25

"I think there's a lot more involved in this than just being a rape artist."

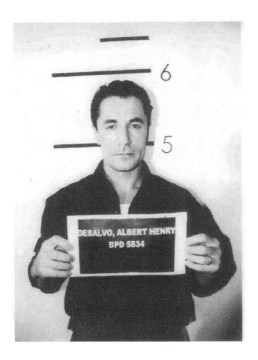

Name: Albert DeSalvo
Nickname: The Boston Strangler
Killings: 13
Location: Boston, MA
Years active: 1962-1964
Fun Fact: DeSalvo claimed he had raped over 1,000 women, once tying up and raping six in one morning.

October 26

"I dreamt of freedom. I had it and lost it through a combination of compulsion and stupidity."

Name: Ted Bundy
Killings: 33-36+
Location: United States (scattered)
Years active: 1969 (possibly as early as 1961) - 1978
Fun Fact: After his escape Bundy used the alias Chris Hagen.

October 27

"I never heard anyone scream like that. She screamed constantly, I kept stabbing and nothing would happen. She kept fighting harder and screaming more. I didn't know... I just ran off."

Name: David Berkowitz
Nickname: The Son of Sam
Killings: 6
Location: New York City
Years active: 1976-1977
Fun Fact: After one murder Berkowitz was seen by a witness as he ran away. He pulled his cap over his face and said, "Oh, Jesus!" as he sprinted by.

October 28

"I gave a confession, I signed it. There's nothing more to add."

Name: Andrei Chikatilo
Nickname: The Butcher of Rostov; The Red Ripper; The Forest Strip Killer; The Rostov Ripper
Killings: 53-56+
Location: Russia
Years active: 1978-1990
Fun Fact: An innocent man named Aleksandr Kravchenko was arrested, found guilty, and executed for the 1978 murder of a 9-year-old girl, which was actually the first murder committed by Chikatilo.

October 29

"She had a rather large forehead and I was imagining what her brain looked like inside, and I just wanted to put (the bullet) right in the middle of that."

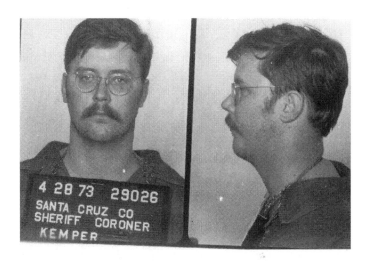

Name: Ed Kemper
Nickname: The Co-Ed Killer
Killings: 10
Location: California
Years active: 1964-1973
Fun Fact: When he was a teenager, Kemper's mom made Ed sleep in a locked basement because she feared that Ed would rape his sister.

October 30

**"I do regret speaking up. . . they had me drugged up
on Thorazine and freezing to death in my jail cell and I
didn't want to live anymore, and I wanted to open up
people's eyes to what was going on in law enforcement,
how they didn't care if they got the right person or not.
I don't think anybody, a human being anyway, could
kill 600 people. I made up some of the worst details
you've ever heard, like how to mutilate a human
being."**

Name: Henry Lee Lucas
Nickname: The Confession Killer
Killings: 3+
Location: United States (scattered)
Years active: 1960-1983
Fun Fact: As a child, Henry was often forced to go to school
barefoot and wearing a dress and curlers.

October 31

"I have a collection of shrunken heads."

Name: Ed Gein
Nickname: The Mad Butcher
Killings: 2+
Location: Wisconsin
Years active: 1954-1957
Fun Fact: When police initially searched his home they found 9 human vulvae in a shoe box.

November

November's featured serial killer is Albert Fish.

Born Hamilton Fish, he later changed his name to Albert, which was probably the last sane decision he made in his bizarre life.

Albert Fish, AKA the Gray Man, the Werewolf of Wysteria and possibly the Brooklyn Vampire, was known in the annals of criminal history as the guy that said: "I like children; they're tasty". However no man is just one thing and, in many ways, Fish was no different from all the other serial killers. Having a taste for the sado-masochistic fetishes, even before the psychiatric community characterized them, Fish was into some serious hardcore fun.

Known for his pain-loving rituals, he would instruct his children and their friends to beat his naked ass with paddles and nail-studded boards. Fish wouldn't let his children stop the beating until he was left in a bloody mess.

Fish's sado-masochistic obsession seemed to germinate from his time in a cruel orphanage where he was beaten mercilessly. It was during this time that he realized his infatuation with perversion.

After his wife left him for another man, Fish seemed to go completely off-the-rails. He preyed on young children, raping and murdering them and began consuming the flesh of his young victims.

Fish once boasted that he had "children in every State," putting the figure at around 100, although it is not clear whether he was talking about molestation or cannibalization, less still as to whether it was true or not. He was a suspect in at least five killings in his lifetime. Fish confessed to three murders that police were able to trace to a known homicide, and confessed to stabbing at least two other people, as well as kidnapping, torturing and castrating a young man who may have been developmentally disabled.

In the end, Fish was put on trial for the kidnap and murder of Grace Budd, and was convicted and executed via electric chair.

November 1

"I plunged the knife into her and it broke. I then finished the job by cutting her throat. I am not sick. I am insane. But that will not stop the game."

(Excerpt from a letter addressed to the Riverside Police Department, Nov. 1966)

Name: Zodiac Killer
Nickname: Zodiac Killer
Killings: 5-28
Location: California
Years active: 1960s-1970s
Fun Fact: The California Department of Justice has maintained an open case file on the Zodiac murders since 1969.

November 2

"When they're dead, they're dead."

Name: George Joseph Smith
Nickname: Brides in the Bath Murderer
Killings: 3
Location: England
Years active: 1912-1915
Fun Fact: All three of his victims were initially thought to have drowned in their bathtubs because of "fainting or having a fit."

November 3

"Because they cried."

(Describing why he favored young virgin girls as victims)

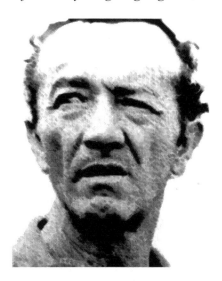

Name: Daniel Camargo Barbosa
Nickname/AKA: Manuel Bulgarin Solis; Beast of the Mangroves
Killings: 72-150
Location: Colombia, Ecuador
Years active: 1974-1986
Fun Fact: In 1984, Barbosa made a daring ocean escape in an old
rowboat from Gorgona prison (known as the Colombian Alcatraz),
where he was imprisoned for raping and killing a 9 year old girl.
Unable to find the boat, authorities declared that he had sunk and
been eaten by sharks. Instead, he made it to Ecuador, where he
immediately began another kill spree, raping and murdering at least
71 girls over the next two years, while living on the streets as a
homeless man.

November 4

"I love to kill people. I love to watch them die. I would shoot them in the head and they would wiggle and squirm all over the place, and then just stop. Or I would cut them with a knife and watch their faces turn real white. I love all that blood."

Name: Richard Ramirez
Nickname: The Night Stalker
Killings: 14
Location: California
Years active: 1984-1985
Fun Fact: Shelley Ramirez was the niece of Richard. When she went to visit him in prison he masturbated in front of her.

November 5

"This thing is not good. It killed my wife."

(Returning a bathtub)

Name: George Joseph Smith
Nickname: Brides in the Bath Murderer
Killings: 3
Location: England
Years active: 1912-1915
Fun Fact: Smith remained legally married to his first wife up until the day he was executed.

November 6

"I want to be able to use a woman whenever and however I want. And when I'm tired or bored or not interested, I simply want to put her away, lock her up in there, get her out of my sight, out of my life."

Name: Leonard Lake
Nickname/AKA: Leonard Hill, Alan Drey, Paul Cosner, many others
Killings: 11-25
Location: California
Years active: 1983-1985
Fun Fact: Lake committed his murders at a rural cabin in the Sierra Nevada mountains, with his partner in murder Charles Ng. They murdered entire young families, keeping the wives alive temporarily as sex slaves. Lake committed suicide by taking cyanide pills just as police were about to arrest him.

November 7

"I feel bad, but I will not turn myself in. I am not stupid."

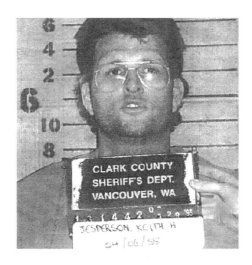

Name: Keith Hunter Jesperson
Nickname: The Happy Face Killer
Killings: 8+
Location: United States (scattered)
Years active: 1990-1995
Fun Fact: Jesperson decided that his long-time girlfriend, Julie Ann Winningham, was interested in him only for money. Jesperson strangled her.

November 8

"I always wondered what it would be like to kill someone."

Name: Gary Ridgway
Nickname: The Green River Killer
Killings: 49-90+
Location: Washington
Years active: 1982-2001
Fun Fact: Before Ridgway's confession, authorities had attributed 49 murders to the Green River Killer. Ridgway confessed to murdering at least 71 victims.

November 9

"I didn't know how to kill, I stabbed her; she looked at me. I stabbed her again. It was terrible."

Name: David Berkowitz
Nickname: The Son of Sam
Killings: 6
Location: New York City
Years active: 1976-1977
Fun Fact: When arrested, Berkowitz was employed by the United States Postal Service.

November 10

"I have had a chance to look at my life from an angle that was never presented to me before. What I did was deplorable. The world has enough misery in it without my adding more to it. Sir, I can assure you that it will never happen again. This is why, Judge Gardner, I am requesting from you, a sentence modification. So that I may be allowed to continue my life as a productive member of our society."

(From a letter to Milwaukee County Circuit Judge William D Gardner)

Name: Jeffrey Dahmer
Nickname: The Milwaukee Cannibal; The Milwaukee Monster
Killings: 17
Location: Wisconsin
Years active: 1978-1991
Fun Fact: Dahmer killed 17 young men of varying ages, all of whom he found physically attractive.

November 11

"Take your worst nightmares, and put my face to them."

Name: Tommy Lynn Sells
Nickname: The Cross Country Killer
Killings: 22+
Location: United States (scattered)
Years active: 1980-1999
Fun Fact: In May 1992, Sells raped, knifed, and beat a woman with a piano stool in Charleston, West Virginia.

November 12

"There is a devil sitting inside me which controls everything."

Name: Anatoly Onoprienko
Nickname: The Beast of Ukraine; Citizen O; The Terminator;
Killings: 52
Location: Ukraine
Years active: 1989-1996
Fun Fact: 26-year-old Yury Mozola became a suspect in several of
Onoprienko's murders. The innocent Mozola was tortured by
Ukrainian secret police for three days, but refused to confess. He
died during the torture. 17 days later Onoprienko was captured.

November 13

"You eat meat with your teeth and you kill things that are better than you are, and in the same respect you say how bad and even killers that your children are. You make your children what they are. I am just a reflection of every one of you."

(From a court statement, 1970)

Name: Charles Manson
Killings: 5
Location: California
Years active: 1969
Fun Fact: Manson was a student of Scientology.

November 14

"I was all hot, just like you're going to blow your head off - like pressure right on you."

Name: Albert DeSalvo
Nickname: The Boston Strangler
Killings: 13
Location: Boston, MA
Years active: 1962-1964
Fun Fact: Before he started killing anyone, DeSalvo would knock on the doors of young women. Carrying a clipboard, he would introduce himself as a representative of a modeling agency and take their measurements. He would promise them that a female representative would contact them later. He never assaulted any of the women.

November 15

"The moment of death is enthralling and exciting. Only those who actually kill know what I mean. Someday, when I am released, I will feel that moment again."

Name: Pedro Alonzo Lopez
Nickname: The Monster of the Andes
Killings: 110-350+
Location: Colombia, Peru, Ecuador
Years active: 1969-1980; 2002-2015?
Fun Fact: Lopez is thought to be the most prolific serial killer in modern history. Because of lenient sentencing guidelines in Ecuador, and despite the discovery of the bodies of more than 50 young girls who were his victims in nearby Peru, he spent only 14 years in an Ecuadoran prison. He was released early "for good behavior." He then spent three years in a Colombian psychiatric hospital. He was released from the hospital in 1998, and disappeared. He is wanted in Colombia for a 2002 murder. His whereabouts are unknown.

November 16

"She was giving me oral sex, and she got carried away... So I choked her."

Name: Arthur Shawcross
Nickname: The Genesee River Killer; The Rochester Strangler
Killings: 14
Location: New York
Years active: 1981-1989
Fun Fact: Shawcross was rumored to have eaten the genitalia of his first victim, 10 year old Jack Blake.

November 17

"When I killed people, I had a desire. This inspired me to kill more. I don't care whether they deserve to live or not. It is none of my concern... I have no desire to be part of society. Society is not my concern."

Name: Yang Xinhai
Nickname: The Monster Killer
Killings: 67
Location: China
Years active: 1999-2003
Fun Fact: Yang would break into rural farmhouses at night, and murder entire families with axes, hammers and shovels, keeping the women alive temporarily to rape them. He was executed in 2004.

November 18

"You know, the head is where everything is at, the brain, eyes, mouth. That's the person. I remember being told as a kid, you cut off the head and the body dies. The body is nothing after the head is cut off. Well, that's not quite true. With a girl, there's a lot left in the girl's body without a head. Of course, the personality is gone."

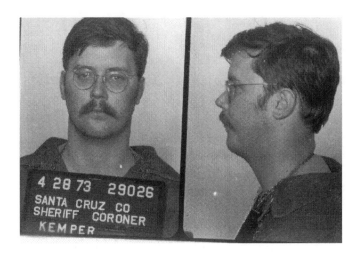

Name: Ed Kemper
Nickname: The Co-Ed Killer
Killings: 10
Location: California
Years active: 1964-1973
Fun Fact: Kemper often kept heads in the trunk of his car.

November 19

"She thinks her shit don't stink. She thinks she's too good for what a woman is made to do – sleep with a man when he wants and needs her and let him do what he wants with her even if she thinks it ain't nice."

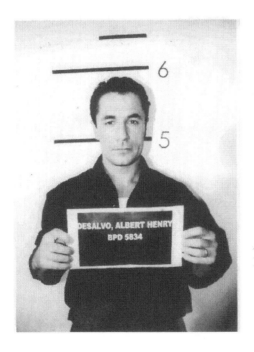

Name: Albert DeSalvo
Nickname: The Boston Strangler
Killings: 13
Location: Boston, MA
Years active: 1962-1964
Fun Fact: Desalvo would often tie a bow under the chin of his victims with the item he strangled them with.

November 20

**"You feel the last bit of their breath leaving their body.
You're looking into their eyes. A person in that
situation is god!"**

Name: Ted Bundy
Killings: 33-36+
Location: United States (scattered)
Years active: 1969 (possibly as early as 1961) - 1978
Fun Fact: Bundy once wrote a pamphlet instructing women on how
to prevent rape.

November 21

"I would usually kill animals for sex. I had sex with them and eventually it got to where I went to human beings."

Name: Henry Lee Lucas
Nickname: The Confession Killer
Killings: 3+
Location: United States (scattered)
Years active: 1960-1983
Fun Fact: His older half-brother and his uncle both introduced him to having sex with animals.

November 22

"I knew I didn't like him."

(About a man he murdered within minutes of meeting him for the first time)

Name: Pedro Rodriguez Filho
Nickname: Pedrinho Matador (Killer Petey)
Killings: 71
Location: Brazil
Years active: 1968-2007
Fun Fact: Filho spent 34 years in prison. During that time, he killed at least 47 of his fellow inmates.

November 23

"Each of us men have married large breast women. My ex-wife is a 39D and yes she was very satisfying to me."

(no pic available)

Name: Robin Gecht
Nickname: The Ripper Crew
Killings: 18+
Location: Illinois
Years active: 1981-1982
Fun Fact: Gecht was a former employee of serial killer John Wayne Gacy. He and three associates were the Ripper Crew, a group of Satanists who mostly killed prostitutes, often cutting off or disfiguring their breasts.

November 24

**"Things I thought would help were turned against me...
I might be on another planet. I don't understand the
gravitational pull."**

Name: John Allen Muhammad
Nickname: The DC Sniper; The Beltway Sniper
Killings: 17+
Location: United States (scattered)
Years active: 2002
Fun Fact: Muhammad spent 17 years in the U.S. Army, before
being honorably discharged with the rank of Sergeant.

November 25

"May your wife and children get raped, right in the ass."

(To the jurors who convicted her)

Name: Aileen Wuornos
Killings: 7
Location: Florida
Years active: 1989-1990
Fun Fact: As a child, Wuornos was repeatedly raped by her grandfather and her grandfather's friends. She became a prostitute at the age of 11.

November 26

"Well, let's just say I can carry cargo better that way."

(Referring to his preference for Volkswagens because the passenger seat can be easily removed)

Name: Ted Bundy
Killings: 33-36+
Location: United States (scattered)
Years active: 1969 (possibly as early as 1961) - 1978
Fun Fact: Bundy was apparently gang-raped by a group of his fellow inmates on death row.

November 27

"The women of Queens are prettiest of all. It must be the water they drink... To the People of Queens, I love you."

Name: David Berkowitz
Nickname: The Son of Sam
Killings: 6
Location: New York City
Years active: 1976-1977
Fun Fact: Berkowitz thought his neighbor, Sam Carr, was a powerful demon.

November 28

"Freedom and technological progress are incompatible."

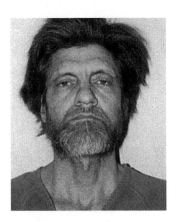

Name: Theodore Kaczynski
Nickname: The Unabomber
Killings: 3 killed, dozens attempted
Location: United States (scattered)
Years active: 1978-1995
Fun Fact: While an undergraduate at Harvard University, Kaczynski was one of 22 unwitting victims in an experiment designed to subject students to extreme emotional distress. The experiment included "vehement, sweeping and personally abusive" attacks, public humiliation, as well as "assaults to their egos, cherished ideas and beliefs." Afterward, they were forced to repeatedly watch videos of their own impotent and helpless responses. The experiment was carried out by notorious professor Henry Murray, and was part of the CIA's MK-ULTRA mind control program.

November 29

"I know it ain't normal for a person to go out and kill a girl just to have sex with her."

Name: Henry Lee Lucas
Nickname: The Confession Killer
Killings: 3+
Location: United States (scattered)
Years active: 1960-1983
Fun Fact: While in prison, Lucas made some really creepy paintings (like the one above).

November 30

"In any matter—job, study, creative work—I give all of myself, but they have repulsed me from my good intentions."

Name: Andrei Chikatilo
Nickname: The Butcher of Rostov; The Red Ripper; The Forest Strip Killer; The Rostov Ripper
Killings: 53-56+
Location: Russia
Years active: 1978-1990
Fun Fact: Chikalito had difficulty maintaining an erection during intercourse.

December

December's featured serial killer is Charles Starkweather.

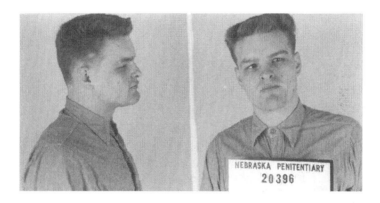

    This guy wanted to be like James Dean. But instead of being a Rebel without a Cause, Charles Starkweather ended up in an electric chair and became a Rebel without a Pulse.

    This young punk with a vicious mean streak, went on a killing spree at the ripe old age of 19 that lasted only two months, but left a wake of blood and a pile of bodies.

    From November 1957 through January 1958, Charlie Starkweather, accompanied by his 14 year old girlfriend, Caril Ann Fugate, murdered 11 people in the states of Nebraska and Wyoming.

    Starkweather's short life wasn't short in turmoil. From an early age to his murderous rampage, his life was filled with pain, rage, anger and distrust. Even though high school friends would recall Charlie as a kind guy, they noted that he could turn on a dime and become a vicious and hate-filled young man with a chip on his shoulder the size of Mount Rushmore.

Starkweather's story and likeness has found its way into literature, films and music. From Bruce Springsteen's Nebraska album to Oliver Stone's Natural Born Killers, Starkweather's mythology played into the modern culture landscape, with the theme of a cold-hearted couple creating havoc in middle America.

But no depiction could illustrate the gruesome and cold-hearted truth of Charles Starkweather. He was executed, via electric chair, a mere 18 months after he was arrested. I guess they executed Charlie quick because someone with this kind of rage shouldn't get a chance to escape.

December 1

"He was a rapist."

(On why he murdered another inmate with whom he was being transported in the back of a prison van)

Name: Pedro Rodriguez Filho
Nickname: Pedrinho Matador (Killer Petey)
Killings: 71
Location: Brazil
Years active: 1968-2007
Fun Fact: Filho had killed 10 people by the time he turned 18.
When he was a teenager, his girflfriend Maria was killed by a gang.
Filho systematically hunted down, tortured and killed at least 8 of
the gang members in an attempt to find out which one murdered
Maria.

December 2

"I don't need to hear all of society's rationalizations. I've heard them all before and the fact remains that what is, is. You don't understand me. You are not expected to. You are not capable of it."

Name: Richard Ramirez
Nickname: The Night Stalker
Killings: 14
Location: California
Years active: 1984-1985
Fun Fact: Ramirez was present the night his cousin Mike shot and killed his wife. Her blood splattered on young Richard's face.

December 3

"You learn what you need to kill and take care of the details. It's like changing a tire. The 1st time you're careful... by the 30th time, you can't remember where you left the lug wrench."

Name: Ted Bundy
Killings: 33-36+
Location: United States (scattered)
Years active: 1969 (possibly as early as 1961) - 1978
Fun Fact: 500 people waited outside the prison to cheer when Bundy was executed.

December 4

"If you love something, let it go. If it doesn't come back, hunt it down and kill it."

Name: Leonard Lake
Nickname/AKA: Leonard Hill, Alan Drey, Paul Cosner, many others
Killings: 11-25
Location: California
Years active: 1983-1985
Fun Fact: Lake had a lifelong obsession with pornography. From an early age, he would take nude photos of his sisters, and use the photos to extort his sisters into having sex with him. Later, he filmed and starred in amateur bondage films. His wife and his long-time girlfriend both left him for this reason. When the killing started, he filmed himself and Charles Ng sexually torturing female victims, leaving behind a trove of evidence as to the depravity of their crimes. Snippets of these films are available online.

December 5

"You got too many girls out there hitchhiking that shouldn't be out there."

Name: Henry Lee Lucas
Nickname: The Confession Killer
Killings: 3+
Location: United States (scattered)
Years active: 1960-1983
Fun Fact: The Texas Rangers brought Lucas to various states to help them "clear" unsolved murders.

December 6

"I hate most prostitutes. I did not want to pay them for sex. I also picked prostitutes as victims because they were easy to pick up without being noticed. I knew they would not be reported."

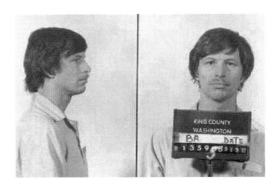

Name: Gary Ridgway
Nickname: The Green River Killer
Killings: 49-90+
Location: Washington
Years active: 1982-2001
Fun Fact: During interviews, Ridgway complained that everyone knew about Ted Bundy but not about the Green River Killer.

December 7

"I like the girls in Ecuador, they are more gentle and trusting, more innocent."

Name: Pedro Alonzo Lopez
Nickname: The Monster of the Andes
Killings: 110-350+
Location: Peru, Ecuador, Colombia
Years active: 1969-1980; 2002-2015?
Fun Fact: Lopez's mother was a prostitute with 13 children. His father was murdered before he was born. Lopez left home when he was 8 years old, and claimed to have been repeatedly raped and molested throughout his childhood and during his first stint in prison as a teenager.

December 8

"People on the outside do not know what evil is."

Name: Arthur Shawcross
Nickname: The Genesee River Killer; The Rochester Strangler
Killings: 14
Location: Upstate New York
Years active: 1981-1989
Fun Fact: While under hypnosis, Shawcross said he was a cannibal in medieval England.

December 9

"The Industrial Revolution and its consequences have been a disaster for the human race."

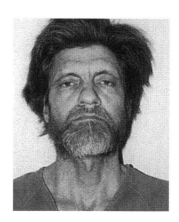

Name: Theodore Kaczynski
Nickname: The Unabomber
Killings: 3 killed, dozens attempted
Location: United States (scattered)
Years active: 1978-1995
Fun Fact: While pursuing the case, FBI profilers believed The Unabomber had a fascination with wood. His bombs were made out of wood. In addition to nails and metal shards, he often included pieces of tree branches and bark as shrapnel inside his bombs. His victims included Percy Wood, Leroy Wood Bearson and Thomas Mosser.

December 10

"For me a corpse has a beauty and dignity which a living body could never hold… there is a peace about death that soothes me."

Name: John Christie
Nickname: The Rillington Place Strangler
Killings: 8
Location: England
Years active: 1943-1953
Fun Fact: Christie raped his last three victims while they were unconscious and continued to do so as they died.

December 11

"Go ahead, take everything I own; take my dignity. Feel good as you grow fat and rich at my expense."

(From a letter to the federal government he wrote before the bombing)

Name: Timothy McVeigh
Nickname/AKA: The Oklahoma City Bomber; Tim Tuttle; Darel Bridges; Robert Kling
Killings: 168
Location: Oklahoma City
Years active: 1995
Fun Fact: McVeigh was awarded the Bronze Star for service in the U.S. Army during the 1991 Persian Gulf War. He claimed that on his first day in battle, he decapitated an Iraqi soldier with cannon fire. Later, he said he was shocked when his superiors commanded him to execute enemy soldiers who had surrendered.

December 12

"You don't take human life like this and sabotage it, like Jesus on the cross. And then say thanks a lot for all the fuckin' money I made off of ya. And not care about a human being and the truth being told. Now I know what Jesus was going through. "

Name: Aileen Wuornos
Killings: 7
Location: Florida
Years active: 1989-1990
Fun Fact: Tyria Moore, who was Aileen's girlfriend, asked her not to tell her too much because she did not want to be an accessory to her crimes.

December 13

"Better to be left to rot on some high hill behind a rock, and be remembered, than to be buried alive in some stinking place."

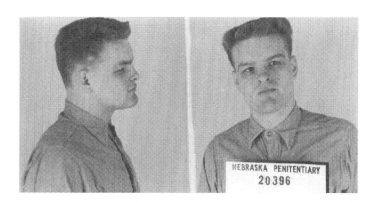

Name: Charles Starkweather
Nickname: Badlands Killer
Killings: 11
Location: Wyoming, Nebraska
Years active: 1957-1958
Fun Fact: After Starkweather was put to death, Nebraska did not execute anyone else for 35 years.

December 14

"I couldn't handle the hate, and the love was actually forced upon me, you know. It was a very strong family-tie type of love."

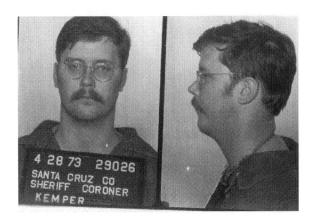

Name: Ed Kemper
Nickname: The Co-Ed Killer
Killings: 10
Location: California
Years active: 1964-1973
Fun Fact: He often had oral sex with his victims' decapitated heads.

December 15

"I have no conscience so that does not worry me. I don't believe in man, God nor Devil. I hate the whole damned race including myself."

Name: Carl Panzram
Nickname/AKA: Jefferson Davis
Killings: 22
Location: United States (scattered)
Years active: 1915-1929
Fun Fact: One of the few things that Panzram purchased (rather than stole) was a yacht. He named the yacht "Alaska."

December 16

"Even psychopaths have emotions. Then again, maybe not."

Name: Richard Ramirez
Nickname: The Night Stalker
Killings: 14
Location: California
Years active: 1984-1985
Fun Fact: Ramirez was a career criminal. He was an accomplished burglar and car thief, and also sold weed to make ends meet.

December 17

"I am in terror!"

(His last words, heard by the executioner)

Name: George Joseph Smith
Nickname: Brides in the Bath Murderer
Killings: 3
Location: England
Years active: 1912-1915
Fun Fact: Smith was hanged on August 13, 1915.

December 18

"I'm gonna kill as many of you as I can. I'm gonna pile you up to the sky."

Name: Charles Manson
Killings: 5
Location: California
Years active: 1969
Fun Fact: Manson once wrote rock star Marilyn Manson a letter.

December 19

"I would cook it and look at the pictures and masturbate."

Name: Jeffrey Dahmer
Nickname: The Milwaukee Cannibal; The Milwaukee Monster
Killings: 17
Location: Wisonsin
Years active: 1978-1991
Fun Fact: Dahmer killed his first victim when he was 18 years old.
He picked up hitchhiker Steven Mark Hicks, brought him back to his
family home, where Dahmer was temporarily living alone, gave him
beer, then hit him over the back of the head with a 10-pound
dumbbell. Later, he masturbated over Hicks's corpse.

December 20

"Every man has his passion; some like whist, I prefer killing people."

Name: Rudolf Pleil
Nickname: The Deathmaker
Killings: 10-25
Location: Germany
Years active: 1946-1947
Fun Fact: Pleil wrote his memoirs in prison. He called them "Mein Kampf."

December 21

"You can cry and stuff, like the rest of them, but it won't do any good. We are pretty – ha, ha – cold-hearted, so to speak."

Name: Charles Ng
Killings: 11-25
Location: California
Years active: 1983-1985
Fun Fact: Ng committed his rapes and murders at a rural cabin in the Sierra Nevada mountains, with his partner in murder Leonard Lake. They murdered entire young families, keeping the wives alive temporarily as sex slaves. Ng has been in prison for 30 years. He is awaiting execution.

December 22

"Last week I went berserk because they slapped me in the head and made terrible noises."

(Speaking about the demons)

Name: David Berkowitz
Nickname: The Son of Sam
Killings: 6
Location: New York City
Years active: 1976-1977
Fun Fact: The street number of where Berkowitz lived has been changed from 35 to 42.

December 23

"I had thought of annihilating the entire block that I lived on."

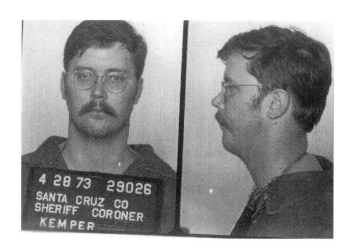

Name: Ed Kemper
Nickname: The Co-Ed Killer
Killings: 10
Location: California
Years active: 1964-1973
Fun Fact: According to profiler Robert Ressler, any 1 out of 10 personality traits can identify someone as a serial killer. Kemper has them all.

December 24

"I actually think I may be possessed with demons. I was dropped on my head as a kid."

Name: Dennis Rader
Nickname: The BTK Killer
Killings: 10
Location: Kansas
Years active: 1974-1991
Fun Fact: Rader was a President of the church council for Christ Lutheran Church and was a Cub Scout Leader.

December 25

"I had been taught by Christians how to be a hypocrite and I had learned more about stealing, lying, hating, burning and killing."

Name: Carl Panzram
Nickname/AKA: Jefferson Davis
Killings: 22
Location: United States (scattered)
Years active: 1915-1929
Fun Fact: When arrested for burglary, Panzram told the officers he had killed too many people to worry about something like that.

December 26

"I have tried to get help for so long and no-one will believe me. I have killed for the past ten years and no-one will believe me. I cannot go on doing this. I also killed the only girl I ever loved."

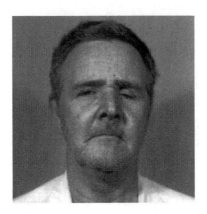

Name: Henry Lee Lucas
Nickname: The Confession Killer
Killings: 3+
Location: United States (scattered)
Years active: 1960-1983
Fun Fact: When his mother didn't like his choice of bride, he killed his mother and raped her corpse.

December 27

"Look over your shoulder. I'm closer than you think."

Name: Keith Hunter Jesperson
Nickname: The Happy Face Killer
Killings: 8+
Location: United States (scattered)
Years active: 1990-1995
Fun Fact: Jesperson's daughter wrote a book called "Shattered Silence: The Untold Story of a Serial Killer's Daughter."

December 28

"None, nothing. No remorse, no nothing. I have a philosophy: the traitor must die."

(When asked whether he felt bad after killing)

Name: Pedro Rodriguez Filho
Nickname: Pedrinho Matador (Killer Petey)
Killings: 71
Location: Brazil
Years active: 1968-2007
Fun Fact: Filho is something of a folk hero to poor Brazilians. He had a tendency to kill other serial killers (most of whom chose defenseless victims), as well as rapists and child molestors. He was released from prison after 34 years, and as of 2015, is still alive.

December 29

"I have got to say this: it felt really good. One the best things I've done in my life."

Name: Daniel Gonzalez
Nickname: Zippy; The Freddy Krueger Killer; The Mummy's Boy Killer
Killings: 4
Location: England
Years active: 2004
Fun Fact: When put in a psychiatric hospital after the murders, he stabbed 6 people in 3 days.

December 30

"When this monster entered my brain, I will never know, but it is here to stay. How does one cure himself? I can't stop it, the monster goes on, and hurts me as well as society. Maybe you can stop him. I can't."

Name: Dennis Rader
Nickname: The BTK Killer
Killings: 10
Location: Kansas
Years active: 1974-1991
Fun Fact: Rader would often wear his victims' underwear.

December 31

"What's one less person on the face of the earth, anyway?"

Name: Ted Bundy
Killings: 33-36+
Location: United States (scattered)
Years active: 1969 (possibly as early as 1961) - 1978
Fun Fact: At one point Bundy was a rape crisis volunteer.

About the Author

"If I heard them call 'soda boy' one more time... I was seriously going to lose it."

(Reminiscing about his time as a soda boy at a broken down bingo hall near the Philadelphia airport.)

Name: johnny trevisani
Nickname: Soda Boy
Killings: 0
Location: Pennsylvania
Fun Fact: johnny's song: "She's Crying at my Funeral" was included in the 2004 feature film "Lost," starring Danny Trejo and Dean Cain.

Since leaving the bingo hall behind, johnny channeled his energy elsewhere, into songwriting and software design.

An accomplished songwriter, johnny wrote and performed for many years, up and down the east coast. Songs like "I Shot My Wife" and "She's Crying at My Funeral" were among the crowd favorites. Fronting the band Furthur Abuse, their album: Avant Gardian Angel was featured on many radio stations across the country and is available on Amazon, iTunes and other online music stores.

He is active in software design, working for many different companies over the years and authoring many apps, including the Serial Killer Quote of the Day apps for iPhone and Android, as well as other apps such as RoboQuote.

johnny is also a licensed private pilot.

Made in the USA
Las Vegas, NV
16 December 2020